LITERACY STRATEGIES FOR
ENGLISH LEARNERS
IN CORE CONTENT SECONDARY CLASSROOMS

MARGARITA ESPINO CALDERÓN

MARIA N. TREJO

HECTOR MONTENEGRO

WITH

ARGELIA CARREÓN

TIMOTHY D'EMILIO

JOANNE MARINO

JOY KREEFT PEYTON

Solution Tree | Press
a division of
Solution Tree

555 North Morton Street
Bloomington, IN 47404
800.733.6786 (toll free) / 812.336.7700
FAX: 812.336.7790

email: info@solution-tree.com
solution-tree.com

Visit **go.solution-tree.com/EL** to download the reproducibles in this book.

Printed in the United States of America

19 18 17   2 3 4 5

Library of Congress Cataloging-in-Publication Data

Calderón, Margarita, author.

    Literacy strategies for English learners in core content secondary classrooms / Authors: Margarita Espino Calderón, Maria N. Trejo, and Hector Montenegro ; Contributors: Argelia Carreón, Timothy D'Emilio, Joanne Marino, and Joy Kreeft Peyton.

        pages cm

    Includes bibliographical references and index.

    ISBN 978-1-936763-21-4 (perfect bound)

    1. English language--Study and teaching (Secondary)--Foreign students. 2. Literacy--Study and teaching (Secondary) 3. Interdisciplinary approach in education. I. Trejo, Maria N., author. II. Montenegro, Hector, author. III. Carreón, Argelia, contributors. IV. D'Emilio, Timothy, contributors. V. Marino, Joanne, contributors. VI. Peyton, Joy Kreeft, contributors. VII. Title.

    PE1128.A2C23 2016

    428.0071'2--dc23

                        2015030468

Solution Tree
Jeffrey C. Jones, CEO
Edmund M. Ackerman, President

Solution Tree Press
President: Douglas M. Rife
Associate Acquisitions Editor: Kari Gillesse
Editorial Director: Lesley Bolton
Managing Production Editor: Caroline Weiss
Copy Editor: Sarah Payne-Mills
Proofreader: Miranda Addonizio
Text and Cover Designer: Rian Anderson

Acknowledgments

We would like to acknowledge the ongoing commitment to English learners and struggling readers by Jeff Jones, Douglas Rife, and our mentor Claudia Wheatley from Solution Tree, as well as the editorial staff from Solution Tree Press. We are most grateful to all the teachers and administrators across the United States who have implemented the ExC-ELL model, and to the associates with Margarita Calderón & Associates who have contributed so much to our learning as we worked together to further develop and refine the ExC-ELL model.

Solution Tree Press would like to thank the following reviewers:

Carie Johnson
English as a New Language Teacher
Scribner Middle School
New Albany, Indiana

Natalie Lower
English Learner Program Specialist
Hayward Unified School District
Hayward, California

Hassan A. Mansaray
Eighth-Grade English Teacher
Edward Middle School
Charlestown, Massachusetts

Norka Padilla
English for Speakers of Other Languages
    Instructional Specialist
Montgomery County Public Schools
Rockville, Maryland

Emily Park-Friend
Seventh-Grade Literacy Skills English
Language Development / Literacy
    Skills Coach
Bruce Randolph School
Denver, Colorado

Erin Ruegg
English Language Learner Content
    Specialist
Isaac School District
Phoenix, Arizona

Visit **go.solution-tree.com/EL** to download
the reproducibles in this book.

TABLE OF CONTENTS

Reproducible pages are in italics.

CHAPTER 4

CHAPTER 5

CHAPTER 6

EPILOGUE

APPENDIX A

APPENDIX B

APPENDIX C

APPENDIX D

APPENDIX E

APPENDIX F

ABOUT THE AUTHORS

 **Margarita Espino Calderón, PhD,** is professor emerita and senior research scientist at the Johns Hopkins University School of Education. She has conducted research, training, and curriculum development for teaching language, reading comprehension, and content knowledge to K–12 English learners. Her work has focused on effective instructional processes, two-way and dual-language programs, teacher learning communities, and professional development for schools with language minority populations and striving adolescent readers. The New York Carnegie Corporation Foundation, U.S. Department of Education, U.S. Department of Labor, National Institutes of Health, and Texas Education Agency have supported Dr. Calderón's research.

A native of Juárez, Mexico, Dr. Calderón is a recognized expert in education with more than one hundred publications to her credit. She is a respected member of several panels and U.S. committees, and she has been welcomed internationally as a visiting lecturer. Dr. Calderón has created and directed her own international institutes for administrators, teachers, and parents. She has experience as a classroom teacher, bilingual program director, professional development coordinator, professor of educational leadership graduate programs, and teacher supervisor.

Dr. Calderón earned a doctorate in multicultural education, applied linguistics, and organizational development through a joint doctorate program at Claremont Graduate University and San Diego State University. Visit www.margaritacalderon .org to learn more about Dr. Calderón's work.

Maria N. Trejo, EdD, is a consultant who provides training, coaching, and instructional leadership support to school and university staff working with English learners, struggling readers, special education students, or gifted and talented education students who are underperforming. She also designs professional development events, webinars, and international teacher exchanges. Dr. Trejo began her professional career as an elementary school teacher. She later taught high school students and prepared teacher candidates at the University of the Pacific and Washington State University. During her thirty-two-year tenure as a consultant and administrator with the California State Department of Education, Dr. Trejo implemented state policies, disbursed funds to improve curriculum and instructional practices, and administered programs to support underprivileged children, underperforming populations, and English learners. She also participated in the development of policies, examinations, and general requirements for state teacher certifications.

Dr. Trejo has participated in state and U.S. education organizations, commissions, boards, and task forces, including the bilingual assessor agencies of the Commission on Teacher Credentialing, Interstate Migrant Education Council, California County Superintendents Curriculum and Instruction Steering Committee, and National Council of States on Inservice Education; she has also served on an Education.com expert panel. Dr. Trejo has contributed to many publications, manuscripts, and articles. Her areas of educational interests are literacy, mathematics, and preschool education.

She earned a doctorate of education from the University of the Pacific in curriculum and instruction, pupil personnel services, and school administration.

Hector Montenegro, PhD, president and CEO of Montenegro Consulting Group, is an associate for Margarita Calderón and Associates. Dr. Montenegro is an internationally recognized keynote and motivational speaker, appearing at conferences, conventions, universities, schools, and special events around the world. He provides training on instructional strategies for English learners and leadership development for administrators and instructional coaches, and he specializes in the teacher coaching process through the use of technology, video recording, web-based platforms, and observation protocols. Dr. Montenegro is also a senior district advisor for the Collaborative for Academic, Social, and Emotional Learning (CASEL) and works with districts on systemic implementation of social and emotional learning.

Dr. Montenegro began his teaching career in San Jose, California, in 1975 where he taught mathematics at the junior and senior high school levels. He later taught and was an assistant principal in Washington, DC, and a junior high principal and a high school principal in Virginia. Dr. Montenegro also served as chief of staff of the District of Columbia Public Schools before moving to Texas, where he served as a principal and an area superintendent in Austin, deputy superintendent for instructional services in Dallas, and superintendent of schools for three school districts in Texas: San Marcos Consolidated Independent School District, Ysleta Independent School District, and Arlington Independent School District. In addition, Dr. Montenegro was an area superintendent for the San Diego School District in California.

He has received numerous awards, including the 2007 National Technology Savvy Superintendents Award, the 2006 Texas Association for Bilingual Education (TABE) Honoree Award for Public Education, the 2006 League of United Latin American Citizens (LULAC) National Distinguished Educator Award for Commitment in Education, the 2006 Texas Computer Education Association Technology Administrator of the Year Award, and the 2005 LULAC National Educator of the Year Award.

He obtained his master's degree from Stanford University and doctoral degree from the University of Texas at Austin.

Argelia Carreón is a lifelong educator. She has taught in Texas, California, Alaska, Washington, and Venezuela, South America. In 1998, she received the TexTESOL I TESOLer of the Year award. Since 2006, Carreón has been an associate with Margarita Calderón and Associates. She served as project coordinator for the 2006–2008 New York City ExC-ELL (Expediting Comprehension for English Language Learners) study funded by the Carnegie Foundation of New York and Johns Hopkins University. Since then, Carreón has also provided ExC-ELL professional development and coaching services in other cities in New York as well as Hawaii, the Marshall Islands, North Carolina, Texas, and New Mexico.

Carreón's experience also includes several administrative and supervisory positions. She served as trainer and then regional manager for the Success For All Foundation in both Brooklyn and Los Angeles. In addition, Carreón is the former director for Bilingual Education and Accelerated Learning for the El Paso Independent School District. As director, she led the bilingual and English as a second language programs for grades K–12 and led parental involvement, migrant education, and Title I schoolwide projects. Her major contribution to education was the design and implementation of the Two-Way Accelerated Bilingual Education program, a unique instructional model that introduced dual-language instruction to the southwestern corner of Texas. Carreón coauthored *The Handbook for the Implementation of the Texas State Plan for Bilingual and ESOL Programs* (1999) and has contributed to numerous publications. She continues to design curriculum and professional development for teaching language and literacy within the content areas.

Carreón holds both a bachelor of science and a master's degree in education; as well as certifications in bilingual education and English as a second language, mid-management, and supervision from the University of Texas at El Paso.

Timothy D'Emilio is a committee member of the National Education Statistics Agenda Committee. From 1991 to 2012, D'Emilio was senior research analyst for the U.S. Department of Education's Office of English Language Acquisition, in which he served as both a grants officer and a contracting officer's technical representative on sponsored research projects and on the department's National Clearinghouse for English Language Acquisition. During that period, he focused on early literacy development, collaborating with the National Center for Education Statistics and the Department of Health and Human Services' Office of Head Start.

Additionally, from 1977 to 1985, D'Emilio participated in the development of preschool reading programs under the supervision of Robert Lado and Theodore Andersson. He served as field coordinator for the Community Services Administration study of the Washington, DC, Hispanic community in 1983 and was assistant to the director of the Office of Bilingual Education for District of Columbia Public Schools from 1985 to 1991.

He completed doctoral coursework in curriculum design and teacher supervision at the University of Pittsburgh in 1982.

Joanne Marino is an educational consultant. She provides professional development, coaching, and leadership support to state departments of education and schools with culturally and linguistically diverse students. Her trainings focus on instructional strategies, assessment, and lesson planning—as well as collaboration within the school and community—in order to develop academic language and raise academic achievement for English learners.

Marino has had a multifaceted career in education as an English as a second language (ESL) and social studies teacher, materials developer, coordinator, and program director. She has taught in the United States and abroad. In 2011, she served as an ESL consultant for North Carolina, where she was responsible for the administration, implementation, monitoring, data collection, and reporting for Title III of the Elementary and Secondary Education Act at the state level; developed and delivered professional development; and provided leadership for curriculum development, curriculum enhancement and support, and program evaluation.

Marino has received several honors, including the 2003 Office of English Language Acquisition Award for Teacher Excellence and Professionalism. She holds a National Board Certification in English as a New Language and was a validator for the National Board for Professional Teaching Standards.

She earned a master's degree in social science and a master's degree in teaching English as a second language from the University of Illinois at Urbana–Champaign.

Joy Kreeft Peyton, PhD, is a research and professional development associate with Margarita Calderón and Associates. She has over thirty-five years of experience working in the fields of languages, linguistics, and culture in education and has worked with teachers and teacher trainers in K–12 and adult education programs across the United States and around the world to improve their instructional practice and study the implementation and outcomes of research-based practice. She serves on a number of project and editorial advisory boards focused on improving education and outcomes for students learning a second language.

Dr. Peyton is also a senior fellow at the Center for Applied Linguistics, a nonprofit organization in Washington, DC, where she served as vice president for sixteen years. Her work with teachers and teacher educators includes providing workshops for teachers of elementary, middle, and high school students on developing the academic language and literacy of students learning English as a second language; working with education leaders in different states to develop sustainable professional development plans for teachers working with students learning English; and teaching courses for university graduate students on phonetics, phonemics, and phonology and on education and human development. She has significant experience as a writer and speaker, with over seventy publications on education issues and numerous presentations at national conferences.

Dr. Peyton holds a master's degree from American University and a doctoral degree from Georgetown University in Washington, DC.

To book Margarita Espino Calderón, Maria N. Trejo, or Hector Montenegro for professional development, contact pd@solution-tree.com.

INTRODUCTION

Gardenia, a ninth-grade student, has difficulties participating in class during oral discussions. She does not have hearing problems, but she is often unresponsive when others speak to her. Her reading and writing are average, although she spends a lot of time looking up words. When she does speak or respond to questions, her vocabulary is limited and simple, and she often replies with one- or two-word answers. Her peers think she is shy or disinterested. In elementary school, she was tested for learning disabilities such as autism, but none were found. Her teachers and counselor can sense her frustration at not being able to converse freely and express herself, and she becomes especially frustrated when she wants to interact with her friends in social settings.

Gardenia did not experience early and continuous oral language instruction; she is one of thousands of long-term English learners (ELs) who have remained limited English proficient for more than six years.

There are over five million English learners—both long-term ELs and newcomers—across all grade levels in U.S. schools (Flores, Batalova, & Fix, 2012). Most long-term ELs are born in the United States, and some are even second- or third-generation citizens. They proceed to middle school still identified as ELs, and some go on to high school as such. Many eventually drop out. Long-term ELs are also relegated to low or limited education in their earlier school years. In fact, the Education Commission of the States (2013) finds that students who remain in EL programs for five or more years perform significantly worse in reading and mathematics than their short-term EL and non-EL counterparts.

Many newcomers—students new to the U.S. education system—also have interrupted formal education. While some newcomers arrive knowing more mathematics and science than native-born students, others come to secondary schools with very limited reading skills. They need interventions and special tutoring to begin catching up with others, yet they bring a host of other skills to the table: resiliency, problem solving, motivation to succeed, and cultural and global understanding. It is important for the U.S. education system to find these positive traits as quickly as possible and provide intensive interventions that address students' specific needs.

The curriculum for ELs needs to offer more exposure to a range of texts and tasks than has been done in the past. While ELs' English instruction is probably limited to five hundred words or less per year, mainstream students—who arrive at school with larger vocabularies to begin with—are learning three to five thousand words each year (Biemiller, 2011; Graves, August, & Carlo, 2011). If ELs are not explicitly taught at least five words a day per subject area, they do not have sufficient vocabulary to comprehend what they read. Furthermore, when they don't read, their vocabularies do not increase.

Moreover, most English as a second language (ESL) teachers, English language development (ELD) teachers, sheltered English instruction (SEI) teachers, and even general classroom teachers prefer to read *to* ELs rather than purposefully teach them how to read the text at hand. Thus, ELs go from grade to grade struggling to comprehend what they pretend to read because they lack basic reading skills. In elementary school, reading tests most likely focus on speed and fluency, meaning teachers rarely diagnose or address a comprehension deficiency by the time ELs reach high school. The Education Commission of the States (2013) reports that U.S. schools have underserved most ELs, and states generally do not monitor students' progress or provide general education teachers with sufficient training to address their needs.

So how do we turn the system around and serve these students? The first step is figuring out exactly how we have failed them.

Why Do We Have So Many Long-Term ELs?

There are many reasons why instruction is not reaching ELs the way it should, from program structures that fail to serve students to practices that are no longer valid. We'll discuss both in more detail here.

Ineffective Program Structures

The most common program structures for language instruction are ESL, SEI, and dual-language instruction.

Most ELs receive only thirty to forty-five minutes of ESL instruction at each grade level. Some are in pull-out programs with an ESL teacher who uses a different curriculum than that of the classroom. This type of ESL instruction often focuses on everyday speech and casual conversation instead of on content or academic discourse. Others receive ESL instruction through a push-in program. When there are many ELs in a classroom, a push-in ESL teacher has to either spend only a couple of minutes with each student or work with all ELs off in a corner, quietly, so as not to disturb the content teacher. Besides not complying with federal law, these ESL programs cannot address all ELs' needs. If ELs are with an ESL teacher for only a few minutes a day, that means they are spending the rest of the school day with core content teachers who may not be adequately prepared to teach them. Is it any wonder they do not make adequate, continuous progress?

Most sheltered English instruction classes tend to use simple decodable texts, which slow the ELs' progress. Simple texts with controlled vocabulary are not rigorous enough to meet core content standards. Mainstream content classes are not effective either when the ELs are not required to read nor held responsible for mastering content and language. In the hundreds of self-contained sheltered mathematics or sheltered science classrooms we have observed, the expectations were low, and the instructional rigor was missing. Student discourse was almost nil. Students' oral language skills might sound almost native in everyday conversation, but the academic discourse is absent. Regrettably, teachers are not teaching the literacy skills students require to become skilled readers and writers (Calderón & Minaya-Rowe, 2011).

For years, the field of second language acquisition has espoused the notion that it takes seven to ten years to become proficient in English. Yet, there is a lack of solid research to support this belief. In fact, the National Literacy Panel on Language Minority Children and Youth (August & Shanahan, 2006, 2008) does not include publications or speeches that promote the concept that it takes so many years to learn English in their reports (Cummins, 1981, 2012; Thomas & Collier, 2002). Many bilingual educators use the concept to justify keeping ELs in bilingual programs for six or more years. While dual-language programs hold great promise for developing bilingual and biliterate students, the results for most leave much to be desired. Ideally, when rigor, high expectations, and quality instruction are the norm, dual-language programs help students perform at grade level in both languages at every grade level. However, studies in Texas (Flores et al., 2012) and from the Education Commission of the States (2013) indicate that staying longer in these programs negatively affects ELs, as most programs suffer a lack of both rigor and preparation for teaching listening, speaking, reading and writing, and content in either language.

The key to making these programs effective for ELs is ongoing professional development for all teachers and administrators that addresses the integration of language, literacy, and content.

Ineffective Practices

According to Tim Shanahan (2013), ineffective reading methods also prevail in U.S. schools. He points out many current practices that are no longer valid.

- Round-robin reading, teachers reading texts to students, teacher-guided reading in small groups, and not giving students texts altogether in subjects such as science

- Reading standards that ask students to describe characters, cause-and-effect relationships, and supporting details without specifying the level of reading complexity and challenge

- Matching students to books instead of having them grapple with challenging texts

- Not giving students challenging books to read

The last ineffective practice has definitely been the trend and mindset for teaching ELs. In fact, the word *differentiation* has unfortunately become synonymous with *watered-down curriculum*—or so much sheltering that teachers do all the work for ELs. No wonder we have so many long-term ELs!

We would add a fifth approach to avoid: silent reading for ELs. We have observed and interviewed students at different grade levels during and after silent reading. They select a book from their assigned bin, sit and turn pages, and pretend to read. When we ask them to tell us what they read, they either try to interpret pictures or have a canned superficial answer. When we dig deeper into the details, inferences, or nuances, they become silent. When we observe adolescents reading silently, we see them going through pages frustrated or disinterested as they wait for a benevolent peer to give them answers to the assignment.

Scaffolding for ELs is important. However, we must admit that the way teachers have traditionally delivered scaffolding has not worked for ELs. Most ESL, SEI, and dual-language instruction teachers use the wrong tools because the methodology for preparing these teachers rarely includes teaching reading comprehension or writing skills along with content-area language. Additionally, dual-language instruction teachers have been taught decoding in the primary language but very little about comprehension building. The major challenge for these teachers is to shift into close-reading methodologies and the types of scaffolding that will push ELs to succeed.

Our traditional approaches tend to set ELs up for failure, but there are ways to fix them! We must use language, literacy, and content in a streamlined, effective way to close this gap and help ELs catch up with their native-English-speaking peers.

How Do We Close the Gap?

A rich language repertoire is key for college and career readiness for all students, and when a student can develop oral and written discourse in two or more languages, he or she is even more prepared. As the world becomes more and more interested in mastering second and third languages, U.S. schools should not lag behind. After all, the United States already has a multilingual and biliterate population, which is a great advantage in developing high levels of language and literacy in two or more languages, either simultaneously from early childhood or in quality structured immersion programs for older students. The United States has evidence-based approaches for both and the available technology. In fact, it even has willing participants and their parents. What it needs is the will power and the courage to implement such programs.

A 2013 trip to China was a wake-up call for us in several ways. We saw how Chinese teacher-training institutions prepare their faculty for developing and using academic English. Previously, these training programs only taught written English, English to simply help students pass the TOEFL test and gain acceptance into U.S. universities, or tourist English. The teacher-training institutions now use academic English to target rich discourse; it is the English of business negotiations, scientific discussions, joint research investigations and publications, and instruction. Isn't this the type of English that we want to develop in U.S. elementary, middle, and high schools? Isn't it time to prepare our own students to be just as competitive? Our ELs are already on their way.

After all, language is the instrument to achieve intellectual, social, and economic success. It is the means to express our ideas and thoughts in speech and writing, and it reflects how we think and learn. Language is what we share to build community. The more languages we speak, the more communities we share. The more words we own to navigate new situations, the better we survive within those situations. What if we teach our students the value of language and how this value is doubled when we can master two or more languages?

Teachers always ask, "What do I need to do to reach my English learners and cover my content and standards?" However, there is no quick fix, especially involving individual teachers working alone to meet all their students' needs. Rather, the way to reach all ELs while covering all content and standards is a meticulous, comprehensive approach that integrates the components of academic vocabulary, discourse, reading comprehension, and writing into all content areas, including mathematics, science, social studies, language arts, and electives.

First, the whole school needs to carefully study what its goals are so that its work aligns with the state standards, determine what it needs to change to reach those goals, and map out how it will make those changes. The standards are powerful tools; Shanahan (2013) states that the standards will likely lead to the greatest changes in reading instruction seen for generations. Second, a professional development program needs to be designed and put in place to address the changes. Third, instructional practices and curriculum adaptations need to dovetail with the standards and the higher levels of rigorous instruction. Fourth, new ways to assess the progress of students, teachers, and administrators will need to align with all of these efforts. The systematic implementation of these processes serves as a context for supporting and assessing everyone in the school.

We want ELs to engage in higher-order thinking and become fully proficient in English and other languages. When teachers collaborate to set up a positive context across all disciplines, students realize that this is the norm in the whole school. Thus, in this book, we offer rigorous learning opportunities specifically for secondary ELs that apply across subject areas, student backgrounds, and approaches to learning language, literacy, and content.

The Framework

As we've seen, it takes a whole-school effort to bring ELs and other underperforming students to high levels of learning. After poring over research, we realized that what works in general instruction coincides with the essential features that ensure success for English learners as well. It turns out that there is consensus about the basic elements of effective instruction, which are in our research studies as well (Calderón, 2007, 2011a, 2012; Calderón, Carreón, Peyton, & Slakk, 2015; Calderón, Hertz-Lazarowitz, & Slavin, 1998; Committee on the Study of Teacher Preparation Programs in the United States, 2010; Slavin, Madden, Calderón, Chamberlain, & Hennessy, 2011). Because these evidence-based studies had larger outcome effect sizes for ELs as compared to the results in the control groups using other instructional approaches, the compilation of these instructional strategies—tested through a grant from the Carnegie Corporation of New York (Calderón, 2007, 2009)—form the foundation of this book.

As you'll see, we use the following framework (table I.1) to plan and deliver lessons.

Chapter 1 solidifies the foundation of classroom structure on which to build this framework. From there, chapter 2 explores vocabulary instruction in relation to both lesson planning and lesson delivery. Chapter 3 looks at reading instruction through the lens of the framework, and chapter 4 explores after-reading instruction. In chapters 5 and 6, we look at literacy in the content areas of mathematics and science, respectively.

We've also included several appendices featuring reproducible handouts to help students understand text features and structures, a summary rubric, three content-area lesson plans, and a reproducible sample lesson plan.

Table I.1: Components of a Comprehensive Lesson for Integrating Discourse Into Literacy and Content Learning

Lesson Planning
1. **Select a core standard and a text that students need to understand and be able to work with for the content taught.** Parse the text to find the sections that contain the information relevant to the standard; discard or don't teach the unnecessary sections of the text. Select a language development standard for ELs. Select authentic and performance assessments.
2. **Select vocabulary, tier one, two, and three words and phrases.** Find complex sentences in the text for pointing out these structures to students, and identify the specific characteristics of the author's craft (features of narrative and expository texts) to serve as models for their writing assignments.
3. **Select a few sentences.** You will use these to model a think-aloud with the metacognitive strategy you have selected (such as comprehending part of a text, understanding an unfamiliar word, or making an inference from a text structure or feature).
4. **Set the context for learning.** Do this with norms and criteria for interaction, types of interaction activities, learning goals and expectations, evaluation processes, expected outcomes, and evaluation of success.

Lesson Delivery
1. **Preteaching of vocabulary:** The teacher chooses five or six key words that ELs need to understand to begin to read a passage, guess what is next in the passage, or to use in their writing.
2. **Teacher read-alouds and think-alouds:** The teacher models the selected metacognitive strategy.
3. **Student peer reading:** Students read for ten minutes with a peer, alternating sentences and stopping after each paragraph to summarize, clarify information, or pose questions.
4. **Peer summaries:** Peers build joint summaries after each paragraph using tier two and tier three words.
5. **Depth of word studies and grammar:** The teacher demonstrates the parts of speech, a compound sentence, or types of words—such as transition words, polysemous words, cognates, root words, and suffixes—using more sophisticated words or words for specificity.
6. **Class discussions:** The teacher poses a question and prompts a discussion involving all students.
7. **Cooperative learning activities:** Teams of students work together to better learn vocabulary and practice discussion skills.
8. **Bloom-type questions and Numbered Heads Together:** Student teams formulate questions from what they read, and the teacher uses these to test other teams for argumentative practice.
9. **Roundtable reviews:** The teacher facilitates timed round-robin-type writing of tier two and tier three words from memory, oral review of key definitions, and oral review of math or science processes or events in history.
10. **Prewrites and drafting:** The teacher assigns reports, short papers, or research papers.
11. **Revision and editing:** The teacher has students rework pieces such as paragraphs, reports, short papers, long narratives, or research papers.
12. **Final products:** Students present the culmination of their work in the form of a speech, project description, or research presentation.

Because these strategies help all students improve, not only ELs, this book is written for secondary teachers of mathematics, science, social studies, English language arts, and electives. ESL, SEI, and dual-language instruction teachers will also benefit, since they most likely team with general education teachers and have to adhere to standards for rigorous English instruction. Administrators and literacy and content coaches will benefit as well. All teachers are language and literacy teachers!

This book is intended for whole-school study groups as schools cope with the reality of higher standards, more ELs, and fewer resources. It attempts to turn old ways of managing schools and classroom instruction into new approaches that dovetail with the unconventionalities, innovations, and novelties of the future.

CHAPTER 1

CLASSROOM STRUCTURES

Traditional classroom structures, especially at the secondary level, have the following characteristics: student desks arranged in rows; teacher-centered, direct (didactic) instruction; ability grouping and tracking; orderly and compliant thinking; disconnected subject areas; and rote learning and memorization. The rigid classroom routines keep students working independently at their seats, limit student-to-student interaction, and eliminate any opportunity for students to gain a deeper understanding of complex language and text through engaging discourse with their peers.

The rapid increase in student populations from diverse socioeconomic, cultural, racial, and language backgrounds has made traditional classroom structures ineffective, as evidenced in achievement data, attendance reports, and low graduation rates. With the rise of accountability, inequities in school districts and in classrooms have become more pronounced, magnifying the achievement gap among subgroups. Unfortunately, in spite of major social and education reforms, social and academic segregation has persisted in schools, and student achievement on standardized measures—especially among ELs—is deplorable. Consequently, orderliness in the traditional classroom can no longer be correlated with effectiveness.

The change of demographics is not the only factor that is making a change in pedagogy and classroom structures essential. Technology has immersed students in the power and influence of social networking and instantaneous access to information. Even though there may be a digital gap, ELs are reaping the benefits of new technologies, whether it be in school or in their home environments. As a result, students are more knowledgeable and comfortable with diversity and globalization, and they welcome new ways of doing work (Pew Research Center, 2007). This generation of learners is less interested in participating in meaningless instructional exercises that have no relevancy or impact on their current reality.

To meet this monumental shift in mindset, ELs need the opportunity to learn in a classroom context that is challenging, content rich, and based on high expectations for academic achievement and that emphasizes social integration and emotional development. A greater focus on inquiry, project-based learning, collaboration, critical thinking, problem solving, and the development of social and emotional skills will better prepare all students—especially ELs—to be college and career ready.

A discourse-rich and highly interactive classroom environment looks significantly different than a traditional classroom. By focusing on developing vocabulary and language functions within the content areas, teachers can further enhance language acquisition by creating multiple opportunities in the classroom for students to practice discourse with their peers. Teachers can also enhance ELs' language proficiency and literacy skills by creating classroom structures that are flexible and that utilize fluid homogeneous and heterogeneous grouping structures. Such an approach facilitates productive discussions, especially when teachers explicitly model for and support students (Alliance for Excellent Education, 2012). The Alliance for Excellent Education (2012) emphasizes the need for an instructional shift to improve the language and content learning of ELs by:

1. Supporting participation in activities that simultaneously develop conceptual understanding of content and language use,

2. Creating opportunities for extended language learning within the content-area classroom, and

3. Exposing students to a more socially engaging process where learners can acquire academic language experientially and where students work and talk together to plan, research, and discuss academic products. (p. 5)

There are several classroom structures that support this shift in learning, including the 4Cs of 21st century skills, social and emotional learning, and cooperative learning.

The 4Cs of 21st Century Skills

The classroom that best prepares ELs for college and careers and meets the pedagogical modifications that the Common Core State Standards (CCSS) require is centered on the 4Cs: (1) critical thinking, (2) communication, (3) collaboration, and

(4) creativity (Partnership for 21st Century Skills, 2014; Pink, 2005; Rotherham & Willingham, 2009).

For example, the classroom that incorporates critical thinking as a regular practice fosters an environment in which ELs can engage in effective reasoning strategies, analyze how parts of a whole interact with each other to produce overall outcomes in complex language systems, and solve problems that relate directly to their learning environment, home environment, and community in innovative ways.

Communication skills have been elevated to a more prominent role as an essential skill to include in all new instructional standards such as the CCSS and other state standards. Communication skills are closely related to and interdependent with collaboration skills. Teachers should not limit them to interactions between the teacher and students but should highlight them in student-to-student and student-to-teacher interactions as well. *Oracy*—being able to express thoughts clearly, articulating opinions through speaking, communicating coherent instructions to different language and cultural groups, and motivating peers through powerful speech—is by far one of the most underrated pedagogical methods in instruction and needs to take its proper place among effective instructional methods, especially for ELs. The business community needs future employees who can communicate clearly and effectively, and this skill set begins with administrators and teachers modeling effective communication.

Developing discourse goes hand in hand with collaborative classroom structures that allow ELs to solve common local or global problems. Students should have the opportunity to work effectively in cooperative groups within the classroom as well as in local and worldwide community service learning activities. Issues such as global warming, health, financial crisis, and even community empowerment require highly developed collaboration skills, and students need to be given the chance to express their ideas and work together on these issues. To help students succeed in these ventures, classrooms need to be dynamic, interactive, and highly engaging learning environments in which all students get to know each other by name and support each other in completing assignments and solving common problems. Collaboration is a critical skill that all teachers and administrators need to strengthen and model at high levels.

In Bloom's Revised Taxonomy, creativity has replaced synthesis at the top of the pyramid (Anderson & Krathwohl, 2001). The Revised Taxonomy defines *creating* as "putting elements together to form a coherent or functional whole; reorganizing elements into a new pattern or structure through generating, planning, or producing" (Anderson & Krathwohl, 2001, pp. 67–68). Creativity and innovation are key drivers in the global economy, and teachers need to be very creative in designing the most effective lessons that will prepare a very diverse population for the 21st century. They need to create exciting lesson plans that are project based, interactive, and collaborative and that use web-based resources. To model creativity, teachers can prepare units that utilize the other three Cs to help students develop leadership skills, increase adaptability, practice teamwork, strengthen interpersonal skills, and practice the art of thinking outside the box of traditional instructional practices. This paradigm shift is difficult for educators to make, but they must change in order to adequately prepare ELs for the challenges of tomorrow. After all, Albert Einstein once said that "imagination is more important than knowledge."

Social and Emotional Learning

The social context in which ELs learn is just as critical as developing the cognitive skills they need to survive academically. Suniya Luthar and Bronwyn Becker (2002) conclude that "raising academic standards without developing students' social-emotional and instructional needs should be both unsuccessful and destructive." In many traditional secondary classrooms, students are passive learners who have minimal interaction with the teacher or their peers. In fact, students often become disengaged with school after fifth grade (Pianta, 2007)—years before they reach the secondary level. This disengagement is because their school experience mostly involves rote memorization, superficial or low-level learning, compliance, stress, boredom, irrelevance, unattainable academic standards, and teachers who don't seem to care (McCombs & Whisler, 1997).

John Bridgeland, John Dilulio, and Karen Burke Morison (2006) find that 70 percent of the dropouts surveyed said they were disengaged from their classes. This effect is multiplied for ELs, who do not understand the language of instruction and have not been afforded the opportunity to interact with either the teacher or their peers. Consequently, educators tend to largely ignore ELs, leading them to withdraw and suffer in silence until they become totally disillusioned with formal education.

Unfortunately, secondary education has served more as a barrier than an opportunity for many English learners. The Alliance for Excellent Education (2012) notes, "Too often, developing language proficiency focuses on 'content-free' tasks isolated from opportunities to hear and learn language from other students and teachers within subject-area classrooms" (p. 4). Language instruction tends to reduce the cognitive demands in secondary-level courses by focusing on using grammar correctly rather than understanding and communicating ideas. It provides limited opportunities for students to speak, read, and write about the content they are learning.

Developments in neuroscience and learning theory point to the fact that a greater emphasis on building a caring community of learners, coupled with high expectations and challenging and engaging opportunities in the classroom, results in students becoming more reflective of their own emotions and relationships. These conditions enhance students' motivation to learn, which is directly linked to academic success (Schaps, Battistich, & Solomon, 2004). Joseph Durlak, Roger Weissberg, Allison Dymnicki, Rebecca Taylor, and Kriston Schellinger (2011) find that school-based universal interventions and their effect in enhancing students' social and emotional learning (SEL) supports the premise that cognitive, affective, and behavior skills are the foundation of academic success. In effect, students are more likely to express their creativity, curiosity, and empathy in environments where they feel included and safe. Students with developed SEL competencies will be better prepared for success in the 21st century.

Since the founding of the Collaborative for Academic, Social, and Emotional Learning (CASEL) in 1994 and the publication of Daniel Goleman's (1995) book *Emotional Intelligence*, the field of social and emotional learning in K–12 education has advanced exponentially (Elias & Arnold, 2006; Elias et al., 1997; Zins, Weissberg, Wang, & Walberg, 2004). According to CASEL (2013), SEL seeks to:

> foster the development of students who are actively engaged in learning; show caring and concern for the well-being of others; and demonstrate higher-order thinking, innovation, creativity and the ability to work toward common learning goals and contribute to the well-being of others and to their school community, all while making strong academic gains. (p. xi)

CASEL (2003) identifies five core SEL competencies that can help EL students strengthen their cognitive, affective, and behavior skills (see also Devaney, O'Brien, Resnik, Keister, & Weissberg, 2006).

1. **Self-awareness:** This is the ability to accurately recognize one's feelings and thoughts and their influence on behaviors, which includes assessing one's strengths and limitations and possessing a well-grounded sense of self-efficacy and optimism.

2. **Self-management:** This is the ability to regulate one's emotions, thoughts, and behaviors effectively in different situations, which includes delaying gratification, managing stress, controlling impulses, motivating oneself, and setting and working toward achieving personal and academic goals.

3. **Social awareness:** This is the ability to take the perspective of and empathize with others from diverse backgrounds and cultures, to understand social and ethical norms for behavior, and to recognize family, school, and community resources and supports.

4. **Relationship skills:** This is the ability to establish and maintain healthy and rewarding relationships with diverse individuals and groups, which

includes communicating clearly, listening actively, cooperating, resisting inappropriate social pressure, negotiating conflict constructively, and seeking help when needed.

5. **Responsible decision making:** This is the ability to make constructive choices about personal behavior, social interactions, and school, which includes considering ethical standards, safety concerns, social norms, the consequences of various actions, and the well-being of self and others.

Explicitly teaching social and emotional skills is essential to meeting state academic standards, especially the Common Core. Teachers need to teach students how to regulate their emotions, problem solve, disagree respectfully, collaborate with their peers, and see others' perspectives (Adams, 2013). Thus, an SEL classroom is one in which teachers develop and maintain a safe, supportive, and well-managed learning environment where students feel cared for, respected, and challenged. This is the type of classroom climate in which ELs flourish.

Interactive, engaging, and participatory instructional methods positively affect student academic performance (Zins, Payton, Weissberg, & O'Brien, 2007). The integration of explicit SEL instruction with the CCSS and other state standards requires a major shift in ELs' language and content-area learning away from the traditional rigid coursework to one that promotes "discourse-rich, experiential learning, in which the learner has opportunities to interact and reflect on information and ideas through observation and inquiry" (August & Hakuta, 1998). ELs benefit greatly when they are able to collaborate with peers to learn academic language.

Aaron Grossman, Torrey Palmer, and Sam Shoolroy (2013) combine the SEL competencies with the CCSS by adopting a framework that engages students in deeply rich and complex text (table 1.1). It is the teacher's responsibility to meet the CCSS expectations (left column) and create a classroom structure that increases the "frequency working with peer groups to examine and problem solve around text" (Chicago Public Schools [CPS], 2012). This approach has the potential not only to incorporate four of the five core SEL competencies by affording students the opportunity to practice these SEL skills but also to help create an inclusive community of learners that is safe for ELs to participate and learn in.

Interestingly enough, the CCSS do not define how teachers should teach these skills, nor do they specify the full range of support for ELs and students with special needs (Sanchez, 2013). Therefore, teachers have flexibility in selecting instructional strategies that integrate 21st century skills with the five core SEL competencies and CCSS.

Table 1.1: CCSS and SEL Framework

Student Experience	Student Needs
Longer Periods of Engagement With Text	• Self-control as they get wiggly (self-management) • Self-motivation to stay engaged with text (self-management) • Perspective as they make meaning of the text (social awareness)
Frustration With Unfamiliar Vocabulary or More Complex Text Structure	• Help if they struggle with longer passages, unfamiliar vocabulary, and structure (relationship skills) • Stress management as they encounter more unfamiliar vocabulary than before (self-management) • Empathy for classmates who are struggling (social awareness)
Increased Frequency Working With Peer Groups to Examine and Problem Solve Around Text	• Self-set goals (self-management) • An understanding of social and ethical norms for behavior when working in peer groups (social awareness) • Cooperative work with peers (relationship skills)

For example, California's English Language Development (ELD) standards for English learners (who comprise a quarter of California's children) are closely aligned with the CCSS for English language arts (ELA). These standards emphasize a change from English as a set of rules about accuracy in grammar and syntax to one in which discourse, text structure, and vocabulary are highlighted in the context of communication and collaboration (California Department of Education [CDE], 2012; see table 1.2, page 16).

In addition, the California grade-level ELD standards identify proficiency levels to help students interact in meaningful ways (Linquanti, 2013).

- **Collaborative:** Engaging in dialogue with others (standards 1–4)

- **Interpretive:** Comprehending and analyzing spoken and written texts (standards 5–8)

- **Productive:** Creating oral presentations and written texts (standards 9–12)

Table 1.2: Key Shifts in the 2012 California ELD Standards

From Conceptualization	To Understanding
English as a set of rules	English as a meaning-making resource with different language choices based on audience, task, and purpose
A traditional notion of grammar with syntax and discrete skills at the center	An expanded notion of grammar with discourse, text structure, syntax, and vocabulary addressed within meaningful contexts
Literacy foundational skills as one size fits all; neglect of linguistic resources	Literacy foundational skills targeting varying profiles of ELs, tapping linguistic resources, and responding to specific needs
Language acquisition as an individual and lockstep linear process	Language acquisition as a nonlinear, spiraling, dynamic, and complex social process
Language development focused on accuracy and grammatical correctness	Language development focused on collaboration, comprehension, and communication with strategic scaffolding to guide appropriate linguistic choices
Use of simplified texts and activities, often separate from content knowledge	Use of complex texts and intellectually challenging activities with content integral to language learning

Source: CDE, 2012.

Similarly, the CPS Department of Pathways to College and Career integrates the CCSS from the state of Illinois and Social and Emotional Learning Standards. The template (table 1.3) illustrates how CPS has aligned the CCSS academic targets with the SEL goals and learning standards, while giving concrete examples of learning activities that teachers are able to incorporate into their lessons. These examples explicitly identify key core SEL competencies. Integrating these activities into daily classroom instruction is a critical step that will ultimately impact ELs' sense of belonging and motivation to do well academically.

Table 1.3: CPS Template Integrating CCSS With SEL Standards

CCSS Academic Targets	Illinois SEL Goals, Learning Standards, and Competencies	Activities
RL.1.4: Identify words and phrases in stories or poems that suggest feelings or appeal to the senses.	**Goals** **31:** Develop self-awareness and self-management skills to achieve school and life success. **Learning Standards** **31A:** Identify and manage one's emotions and behavior. **Competencies** **Self-awareness:** The ability to accurately recognize one's feelings and thoughts and their influence on behaviors	**Purpose:** Students extend their feeling vocabulary and understand that authors choose specific words to express a range of feelings. **Learning activities:** Activate vocabulary knowledge using role play or a word splash. Have students connect their own feelings to those in the story or poem.
RI.5.3: Explain the relationships or interactions between two or more individuals, events, ideas, or concepts in a historical, scientific, or technical text based on specific information in the text.	**Goals** **32:** Use social awareness and interpersonal relationship skills to establish and maintain positive relationships. **Learning Standards** **32A:** Recognize the feelings of others. **32B:** Recognize individual and group similarities. **32C:** Use communication and social skills to interact effectively with others. **32D:** Demonstrate an ability to prevent, manage, and resolve interpersonal conflicts in constructive ways. **Competencies** **Social awareness:** The ability to take the perspective of others from diverse backgrounds and cultures and to understand social and ethical norms for behavior **Relationships skills:** The ability to establish and maintain healthy and rewarding relationships with diverse individual and groups	**Purpose:** Students will explain the relationships or interactions from the information in the text and how it influenced the historical event. **Learning activities:** In a social studies lesson about the first time early explorers of the North American continent met Native Americans, students discuss how feelings of both groups (such as curiosity, anxiety, and fear) might have affected the way they treated each other. In pairs, students discuss a time in their own lives when they met someone new, how they felt, and how their feelings affected their behavior and their relationship. In a large group, students discuss how feelings affect behavior and how behaviors affect relationships. Then, the teacher asks, "How could the way early explorers and Native Americans treated each other initially affect their relationships with each other, and how did this ultimately affect history? Could anything have been done differently to improve the way the relationship developed?"

continued >

CCSS Academic Targets	Illinois SEL Goals, Learning Standards, and Competencies	Activities
W.9–12.7: Conduct short as well as more sustained research projects to answer a question or solve a problem; narrow or broaden an inquiry when appropriate; synthesize multiple sources on the subject, demonstrating understanding of the subject matter under investigation.	**Goals** **31:** Develop self-awareness and self-management skills to achieve school and life success. **33:** Demonstrate decision-making skills and responsible behaviors in personal, school, and community contexts. **Learning Standards** **31C:** Demonstrate skills related to achieving personal and academic goals. **33B:** Apply decision-making skills to deal responsibly with daily academic and social situations. **Competencies** **Self-management:** The ability to regulate one's emotions, cognitions, and behaviors to set and achieve personal and educational goals **Responsible decision making:** The ability to make a realistic evaluation of the consequences of various actions	**Purpose:** Students will demonstrate self-management and responsible decision-making skills in completing a rigorous writing task with multiple sources of information. **Learning activities:** Have students choose a question or problem to solve and submit a plan with goals and timelines for completing this writing task. In small groups, after completing the research on the subject, invite students to defend their choices of sources in answering their question or solving the problem.

Source: National Governors Association Center for Best Practices [NGA] and the Council of Chief State School Officers [CCSSO], 2010b.

Cooperative Learning

One of the most effective and easy-to-implement classroom structures is cooperative learning, which promotes participation and facilitates the creation of a community of learners that includes ELs at all language proficiency and academic achievement levels. If done well, cooperative learning improves classroom management and enriches social interactions while preparing students for college and careers in reading, writing, speaking and listening, and language. Cooperative learning allows teachers to form small teams of mixed-ability students. These team members work together using a variety of learning activities to improve their understanding of different subject areas and language skills (Calderón et al., 1998). Researchers agree that ELs progress much quicker when they work in small-group settings, have multiple opportunities to practice new language, and are engaged in interesting work (Calderón, 2007).

Cooperative structures that teach and support students in learning the five core SEL competencies and skills are just as critical as teaching content; consequently, they deserve a rightful place in developing the scope and sequence of lesson plans. After all, interaction is the basis for learning (Donovan & Bransford, 2005).

Defining Protocols and Norms

Teachers who swear by cooperative learning carefully set up group work norms (the dos and don'ts of behaviors) and the proper discourse for working with peers during different activities and strategies for learning. Teachers convey that learning is the goal for every task assigned to students, not the activity itself. The goal is not a product and not busywork. It is to make sure that all team members have mastered the concepts. Students thrive during these opportunities for mastery and appreciate that the teacher has orchestrated a safe and studious context. The teacher constantly monitors and facilitates student interaction and learning. Cooperative learning is also a good opportunity to collect more authentic performance or assessment data.

The seven-step process for orchestrating positive cooperative learning experiences is as follows.

1. Set up the protocols for collegial discussions.

2. Post the norms of interaction.

3. Write the total time to conduct each activity.

4. Model how to work in pairs, triads, and teams of four.

5. Present rubrics for self-assessment and team assessment.

6. Select the social skills and collaborative discourse protocols to model for students.

7. Determine how to assess teamwork, individual performance, and the quality of student products and how to set goals for working together more effectively the next time.

Students should collaboratively develop protocols and norms that everyone agrees to. The teacher can then post them in the classroom as a reference when needed (see examples in figure 1.1, page 20). We encourage teachers to regularly reinforce these mutually agreed-on practices to strengthen students' collaborative skills. It is important that they share a common language regarding expected behaviors and procedures.

Norms	Protocols
• Everyone contributes ideas.	• Respect others.
• Everyone has a specific task (not role).	• Be positive.
• Everyone learns from one another.	• Accept opinions.
• Everyone works with an open mind.	• Contribute to the discussions.
	• Help others.
	• Accept help.
	• Stay on task.
	• Accept responsibility.

Source: Calderón et al., 2015.

Figure 1.1: Sample student-created social norms and protocols in cooperative learning.

Embedding the five core SEL competencies into the social norms and protocols will further enrich the motivation to learn and strengthen the learning community of the classroom. Explicit instruction and modeling of the SEL competencies will add depth to the cooperative learning discourse and content-based exercises.

According to David Johnson and Roger Johnson (1987, 1991), five conditions must be in place in order for cooperative efforts to be productive. These include the following.

1. **Positive interdependence:** Each team member's efforts are required and indispensable for team success, and each member contributes to the joint effort.

2. **Face-to-face interaction:** Students come together to explain orally, teach one another, and check for understanding.

3. **Individual and group accountability:** Accountability prevents social loafing, as each student makes an active contribution to the team.

4. **Interpersonal and small-group skills:** Students develop social skills for leadership, decision making, and trust building.

5. **Group processing:** Students reflect on how well they are working together and how they might do better as a learning team.

When these conditions are the norm, it is easier to integrate cooperative learning strategies into daily classroom activity. For instance, CASEL (2013) identifies several interactive and cooperative learning approaches, such as brainstorming, discussion, games, role plays, and problem-solving strategies. Such activities engage students in an active learning experience and create a learning environment where caring, responsibility, and a commitment to learning thrive.

Similarly, the ExC-ELL (Expediting Reading Comprehension for English Language Learners) Model uses an observation protocol, which documents classroom observations, provides coaching support, and includes five cooperative learning strategies that also promote active engagement in learning and the development of SEL competencies (Calderón, 2013).

1. Teach and display discourse protocols and behaviors for cooperative learning.

2. Use a variety of strategies to practice academic language and content knowledge.

3. Explain, model, and monitor team learning behaviors and social skills.

4. Ensure all students participate during interactive learning.

5. Have students use self-assessments for social and emotional skills and productivity.

Unfortunately, teachers at the secondary level do not engage students as frequently as they can. Many find it challenging to get off script and turn the responsibility of learning over to students by fostering an engaging, interactive, and academically driven learning environment. This change in practice is difficult, especially for teachers who have not seen or been trained in alternative ways of teaching and classroom management that address the needs of ELs. Teachers may see such a radical change from the way they have been taught and the way they have been teaching for years as a risky proposition. There's always a fear that it could get messy, exhausting, and chaotic (Sanders, 2012). Yet, learning is the purpose of cooperative learning strategies, and every student should be held responsible for his or her individual performance and his or her contributions to the group goals and final products.

Before teachers are trained on ExC-ELL, our team of coaches often observes teachers asking students very low-level recall questions, speaking much more than students do, using direct whole-classroom instruction to deliver lessons, and involving only one or a few students at a time. Cooperative learning will go a long way toward helping teachers engage ELs in the classroom while also learning the academic content in English.

Providing a Safe Space Through Cooperative Learning

As noted in the introduction, some students who enter school behind their peers will have smaller vocabulary bases. One way to build vocabulary is to use cooperative learning to help ELs interact in groups or teams with more capable peers. Peers provide a safe context for ELs to try out their new language in small groups.

The goal of working in teams should be individual accountability for mastering specific language and content. ELs should be armed with prompts, discussion frames, question starters, and sentence starters for these carefully crafted conversations. Peers can also translate or explain a task or content to ELs, but only when absolutely necessary. That peer must also provide the English words, phrases, and sentences that the EL will need to use to describe, answer, or pose a question when it is time to participate in discussions in English.

It's important to note that more than four students on a team might provide a negative rather than positive experience, because ELs can find a place to hide, and peers are willing enablers of these coping mechanisms. On the other hand, when there are fewer students working together on a task or the task can be subdivided into smaller tasks, ELs have no place to hide and must rise to the occasion and participate (Calderón, 2011a).

Summary

The rapid increase in student populations from diverse socioeconomic, cultural, racial, and language backgrounds and the daily access to technology that provides students with social networking and immediate information have made traditional classroom structures ineffective, as evidenced in achievement data, attendance reports, and low graduation rates. This chapter has presented considerations for providing ELs with opportunities to learn in classrooms that are challenging, content rich, and based on high expectations for academic achievement and that emphasize social integration and emotional development. We've outlined a proposed shift to inquiry, project-based learning, collaboration, critical thinking, problem solving, and the development of social and emotional skills to help all students—especially ELs—be college and career ready.

CHAPTER 2

TEACHING VOCABULARY

At the most basic level, *oral language* means communicating with other people. But when we talk about academic oral language development across the curriculum, we mean not just teaching students to speak but, even more importantly, improving their ability to communicate more effectively. At higher academic levels, effective speech and communication involve thinking, content knowledge, and skills development—which require a context for continuous practice and training. Thus, in our work with schools, we define *academic language* as a combination of words, phrases, sentences, and strategies needed to participate in class discussions, to understand and express complex concepts in texts, and to express oneself in academic writing.

In this chapter, we discuss the importance of academic discourse, oracy, and conversations as well as ideal contexts for collegial discussions in classrooms before jumping into the lesson planning portion of the framework. After discussing the four steps of lesson planning, we explore the first step of lesson delivery: the preteaching of vocabulary.

Academic Discourse, Oracy, and Conversations

State standards emphasize the development and use of academic discourse, oracy, and conversations. The Common Core State Standards clearly facilitate student interaction with and development of academic language; they mention the word *vocabulary* over two hundred times. Also, the anchor standards for Listening and Speaking address the domains of Comprehension and Collaboration and Presentation of Knowledge and Ideas. Each has subcategories defining what a student should understand and be able to do by the end of each grade. Consider these goals for seventh grade (NGA & CCSSO, 2010a):

- Engage effectively in collaborative discussions (one on one, in groups, and teacher led) with diverse partners on topics, texts, and issues, building on others' ideas and expressing their own clearly

- Come to discussions having read the text

- Recount or describe key ideas or details from text

- Ask and answer questions about what a speaker says, summarize what a speaker says, acknowledge new information, modify own views

- Tell a story or recount an experience, summarize a written text

- Plan and present an argument that supports claims

Having opportunities to participate in discussions is critical for ELs. For the most part, they are left out because their English is limited. The contrary should be the norm—the more limited the English of students, the more participation opportunities they should have.

Some students who enter school behind their peers will have smaller vocabulary bases of common tier one and tier two words. According to David Coleman and Susan Pimentel (2012), "materials . . . and instruction must address this vocabulary gap early and aggressively . . . including providing more instruction for students with weaker vocabularies rather than offering them fewer words than their peers" (p. 3). The *learning* in cooperative learning should be the outcome each time students interact in groups or teams with more capable peers.

Teacher oral presentations about a topic serve to model the type of language required to discuss that topic. But only listening to a teacher speak without the students reading and using the language for that topic themselves is insufficient. Students must listen, speak, read, and write in order to own the content and the discourse for that content. Teachers should assign rigorous tasks to ELs that will stretch their proficiency and hold them accountable for using new English words, phrases, and sentences that were taught by the teacher for this purpose. The teacher should also clarify that the goal of working in teams is individual accountability for mastering specific language and content. ELs must be armed with prompts, discussion frames, question starters, and sentence starters for these carefully crafted conversations.

Another resource for ELs is a peer who can take on the important role of translating or explaining a task or content. However, as noted earlier, that peer must also provide the English words, phrases, and sentences so the EL can describe, answer, or pose a question during discussions in English.

Discourse

The key to oral language development is to focus instruction on strategies that build listening comprehension and oral expression from the first day that students arrive in class. This is especially critical for ELs who come to school with small vocabularies, as discussed in the introduction, because that places them years behind their peers (Hart & Risley, 1995). Oral skills involve vocabulary, grammar, pragmatics, *and* discourse. Unfortunately, teachers spend considerable time teaching isolated words and some grammar but often overlook discourse.

Discourse is a combination of sociocultural, metacognitive, and metalinguistic skills and can be any of the following.

- A formal discussion of a topic in speech or writing

- An informal conversation

- Socially acceptable ways of using language (saying the right things at the right time or expressing values and one's own thinking)

- Expository and narrative writing (dialogue, monologue, descriptive, argumentative, multimedia, essay, poem, or research paper)

Oracy

Oracy is also a combination of sociocultural, metacognitive, and metalinguistic skills. Oracy is dependent on the words explicitly taught at the beginning of a lesson and used throughout the lesson in peer and teacher discussions and writing activities for that lesson. Gardenia, whom we met in the introduction, did not experience this type of early and continuous instruction. Hence, she is one of thousands of long-term ELs who have remained limited English proficient for more than six years.

Conversations

Carefully crafted conversations entail a process that is sequential and concurrent. Language and literacy are developed in tandem. Words and any associated skills are not learned in isolation or devoid of context; rather, academic vocabulary and oracy are developed in the processing of texts that are being read. Essentially, teachers must develop coherent writing and specific writing skills while teaching vocabulary through the texts that students are reading (see figure 2.1, page 26).

Well-Taught Vocabulary ⟶ Oracy ⟶ Reading Comprehension ⟶ Cohesive Writing ⟶ Academic Achievement

Figure 2.1: The process of creating carefully crafted conversations.

It is important to teach students the words that we want to hear in their speech during class discussions and see in their writing. While this chapter elaborates on listening and speaking with instructional examples for each of those components, oracy and discourse are emphasized throughout each chapter using a variety of instructional strategies.

The Context for Collegial Discussions

There are many opportunities for secondary students to engage in high-level conversations in student teams, one on one, or in a whole-class format that meet the requirements of state standards. For example, consider the following occasions.

- High-quality, text-dependent *questioning* that leads to reformulation of assumptions, clarification of information, or prediction of possible outcomes

- Oral *debates* for which students prepare background, details, positions, citations, cohesive arguments, and conclusions

- Oral *speeches* in which students present information in a limited time frame in performances that require a beginning, middle, and end; are sequential, informative, and interesting; and hold the audience's attention

- Oral *presentations* of key information requiring students to know key facts, read the audience, be aware of time and tone, and use specific relevant vocabulary

- Oral *interviews* for jobs, scholarships, internships, or other situations, where students need to convince the audience of their skills and potential

- *Advertising copy*, where students need to sell both the merits of a product or service and their personal expertise with and knowledge of it

- *Role plays* in which a student may be asked to portray a police officer, attorney, clergy, counselor, painter, architect, athlete, scientist, or university professor

These activities require students to be knowledgeable of a topic in order to reiterate what they learned; affirm their knowledge; analyze, summarize, or synthesize information; restate facts; provide conclusions; and provide points of view. These are common skills across the content areas that educators must explicitly teach to English learners and many other students. ELs benefit greatly from additional guided practice, corrective feedback, and systematic instructional sequences (Crawford-Brooke, 2013).

Two of the best ways to teach these skills are for the teacher to model the skill to be learned in the class period and for students to interact with peers using that approach (Calderón et al., 1998).

Lesson Planning

All of the facets of instruction described previously can be included in carefully planned lessons. Lesson development begins with four considerations.

1. **Select a core standard and a text that students need to understand and be able to work with for the content taught:** Parse the text to find the sections that contain the information relevant to the standard; discard or don't teach the unnecessary sections of the text. Select a language development standard for ELs. Select authentic and performance assessments.

2. **Select vocabulary, tier one, two, and three words and phrases:** Find complex sentences in the text for pointing out these structures to students, and identify the specific characteristics of the author's craft (features of narrative and expository texts) to serve as models for their writing assignments.

3. **Select a few sentences:** You will use these to model a think-aloud with the metacognitive strategy you have selected (such as comprehending part of a text, understanding an unfamiliar word, or making an inference from a text structure or feature).

4. **Set the context for learning:** Do this with norms and criteria for interaction, types of interaction activities, learning goals and expectations, evaluation processes, expected outcomes, and evaluation of success.

Select a Core Standard and a Text

Because large pieces of text will be difficult for ELs initially, teachers can parse the text to select sections to read that contain key information. To do this, teachers will want to answer the following questions:

- Which sections of the text address the standard?

- Which include extemporaneous or filler information in a textbook and can be overlooked?

- Which include basic information to build on?

- What content standard does the text address?

- What literacy and academic language standard can be worked in with this content standard?
- What is the English language development standard for the different levels of ELs in this classroom?

Once the standards are selected, plan how students will be assessed for vocabulary, reading, writing, and knowledge of content.

Select Vocabulary and Phrases

The next step is to select five or six tier one, two, and three words and phrases to preteach before approaching the topic or the text. More words can be taught during and after reading. The teacher must determine which words and phrases students will need to know in order to discuss the text and to use in their writing later on.

While it's easy to end up with a long list of words for each category of words, teachers must be strategic. More words can be taught during and after reading. These criteria will help teachers reduce their lists considerably.

- Words and phrases you want to hear in their discussions
- Words and phrases that are important and useful for understanding the text, the concept, and the knowledge to master
- Words, phrases, and sentence structures that have instructional potential for enhancing reading and writing skills and language learning
- Words, phrases, and sentence structures you want to see in students' short and long pieces of writing

Let's take a moment to look at the three tiers of words.

Tier Three Words

We will start with tier three words and phrases, since those are the ones highlighted in textbooks and found in the glossary to texts. This category includes infrequently used academic words and subject-specific words that label content discipline concepts, subjects, and topics. They are sometimes called technical words and are key when learning specific subjects.

Students are often held accountable for tier three words on exams. However, exams are not the reason to focus on tier three words. As articulated clearly in the standards, all students need to come to discussions prepared by having read or researched the material under study; being able to refer to evidence on the topic, text, or issue; and probing for and reflecting on ideas under discussion. ELs can participate in these rich discussions when teachers select key words to preteach from the text.

Some examples of tier three words in science are *photosynthesis, hibernation, stored energy*, or *osmosis*. In social studies, tier three words include *democracy, Boston Tea Party, legislative body*, or *medieval wars*. In mathematics, *perimeter, hexagon, proper fractions*, and *improper fractions* are tier three words.

Tier Two Words

This category of words includes information-processing words that nest under tier three words, particularly in long sentences: polysemous words; transition words and phrases, sentence starters, and connectors; more sophisticated words for rich discussions and specificity in descriptions; and idioms and figurative language.

For rich discussions, tier two words and phrases need to be pretaught along with tier three words. Tier two words help make sense of the tier three words. In fact, it is more important to preteach tier two words for comprehending the concepts and applying them in discussions as tier three words will often be redundant. That is, words such as *photosynthesis* and *legislative* will be repeated several times in a text, and pictures often add to the comprehension of the concept. Tier two words and phrases, on the other hand—such as *in spite of, over the course of, thus, thereby, notwithstanding*, or *henceforth*—may appear only once or twice in the text, but they signal important turns, milestones, or key pieces of information. Often, they hold the definition of a concept together. There are several subcategories for tier two words, and the textbooks and texts that teachers use will have many more. Here are some examples that will help guide the selection from any classroom text.

Look for the following to indicate a tier two word.

- **Polysemous words (words with multiple meanings):** At first glance, they seem like very easy words. We are accustomed to these words in various contexts, but ELs do not know all the meanings of words. Consider *trunk*; it could be part of an elephant, the upper torso, a large chest, the back of a car, truncated numbers, or swimming trunks. Many polysemous words look like very simple everyday words, such as *saw, leg, fall, left, right, court, light, right, check, hand, rest, roll, table*, and *round*. However, think of all the meanings for each and all the idioms they are found in.

- **Transition words and connectors:** This category includes words that often connect and define the relationship between clauses, such as *due to, because, for this reason, therefore, thus, and, or, since, so that, in contrast, nevertheless, moreover, likewise, in addition, in particular, such as, for example, as well as, for instance, however, in order to, by the way, subsequently, initially, thereafter, afterward*, and *in conclusion*.

- **Sophisticated words or words for specificity:** This grouping includes more specific phrasing than might be found in nonacademic speak. For example, instead of always using the verb phrase *to say*, a more precise choice might be *verbalize, dialogue, debate, vocalize, articulate, announce, specify, discuss, describe, proclaim, comment, mention, communicate, argue, request, remark*, or *reveal*.

- **Information-processing words (noun, verb, adjective, adverb forms):** Some of the most common groupings in this category include: *summary/ summarize, infer/inference, argue/argument/argumentative, predict/prediction, synthesize/synthesis, observe/observation, approach/approaches, body* (of research), *display* (noun, verb), *generate, accuracy/accurate, apparent/ apparently, arrange, circle* (verb), *distinct/distinction/distinguish, depict, delineate, criteria, assumption, belief, crucial, effect*, and *affect*.

- **Cognates:** This classification involves words that have the same linguistic derivation in different languages (like English and Spanish), such as *hypothesis/hipótesis, observations/observaciones, classification/clasificación, tentative conclusions / conclusions tentativas, evaluate/evaluar, process/proceso, president/presidente, club/club, fantastic/fantástico*, and *algebra/álgebra*.

- **Clusters, phrases, idioms, and figurative language:** This category includes phrases that most likely will not translate into a comprehensible phrase in another language, such as *once in a while, over the course of, no foot to stand on, landed on both feet, break a leg, set the stage, foot in mouth disease, on the one hand, on the other hand, if and when, talk in circles, talk of the town, on the same page, on the right track, map out your strategy*, and *draw some conclusions*.

Tier One Words

Tier one words are those easy, everyday words known by all English-dominant students by second grade but not necessarily known by a high school newcomer EL. Some older students do not recognize the pronunciation of a word because they have only read it (such as *shift, ship, chip*). Others do not recognize it because they have only heard it (such as *tough, toothache*).

Many recent newcomers from Africa, the Middle East, or Central America may not have the background knowledge for certain words, such as *parka* or *blender*. That said, the ubiquitous nature of technology has made the world a little smaller. When a colleague of ours visited schools in rural Chile with scant resources, he was astonished when students took out their smartphones to take a picture of him. They all had Facebook pages and were well aware of world events. So, while newcomers to the United States may understand the concepts, they may not have the English labels yet. Thus, tier one words are probably the most difficult to select, because teachers don't know which words students don't know. It is a good idea to give students the opportunity to write words they don't know on post it notes as they encounter them in texts and drop these notes in a box for the teacher to explain later. Most tier one words can be taught quickly through pictures, drawings, or gestures.

In diverse and mixed-ability classes, all students will benefit from instruction on different types of words. Even non-ELs need specificity of definitions and practice using them with precision. For instance, during partner reading, students will probably work with words on their own. It is important to give the correct definition of the words during or after reading. If their list of unknown words is too long (such as thirty words or so for a half page of text), the text is too difficult for the ELs in your class. In these situations, teachers can arrange for additional intensive intervention to help their language accelerate.

Select a Few Sentences

Each text provides an opportunity to teach a reading comprehension or metacognitive strategy and to teach academic grammatical structures specific to a discipline (such as cause and effect, rereading a sentence for comprehension, making inferences, self-correction, and using context clues). These strategies and structures can be taught through by modeling through a think-aloud. First, teachers should select a few sentences that appear important or prevalent in the text. The teacher then reads these sentences aloud and describes what each sentence is saying using sentence stems like the following.

- "This sentence is saying that . . ."
- "One important fact here is . . ."
- "I'm not sure what this word means, so I'm going to write it down and look it up or ask someone . . ."
- "This seems to be the main idea. Let me read it again. It says . . ."
- "To summarize these three sentences . . ."

Next, the teacher asks the students to describe what he or she was modeling. Based on their responses, the teacher can clarify the strategy if necessary. Then, the teacher gives them a copy of the sentence starters and asks them to apply the strategy during partner reading. When they do their partner reading, the teacher walks around to hear the accuracy of their application.

More examples for think-aloud prompts include the following.

- (After reading a sentence) "The cause is here on the first line."
- "The effect is on the third line."
- "Based on . . . , the effect of . . . on . . . is . . ."
- "The evidence in this line confirms the information on . . ."

All sentence stems can be typed and distributed to students or pasted on table tents before they begin their partner reading.

Set the Context for Learning

Interaction is the basis for learning (Donovan & Bransford, 2005). Teacher-student and student-student interaction is the most powerful tool for learning. Cooperative learning can be a blessing or a catastrophe for interaction! Teachers who swear by it set up the norms of cooperation (the dos and don'ts of behaviors discussed in chapter 1) and the proper discourse for working with peers during different activities and strategies for learning. Teachers convey that learning is the goal for every task assigned to students, not the activity itself. The goal is not a product and not busywork—it is to make sure that all members of the team have mastered the concepts. Students thrive during these opportunities for mastery and appreciate that the teacher has orchestrated a safe and studious context. The teacher constantly monitors and facilitates the interaction and learning. It is also a good opportunity to collect more performance or authentic assessment data.

One strategy teachers like to use is to assign each team a norm and ask students to put together a three-minute role play about it. For example, they first role-play a negative exemplar—a bad behavior or a representation of a norm portraying someone who doesn't want to accept help. Then, they role-play a positive exemplar of someone who accepts help graciously. This should only take about twenty minutes the first or second day of the semester, but the benefits will remain for the rest of the year. Students need to see what is good behavior or bad behavior and experience how it feels, even if they are pretending as they role-play. Occasionally, students need to self-assess their performance in pairs or teams. They can simply fill in the blanks on exit passes, such as "We did well on _____ but need to improve on _____."

Table 2.1 provides suggestions for ways to observe students as they work in cooperative learning groups.

Table 2.1: Observing Cooperative Learning

Task	Prompt
Cooperative Task	Are all students on task? Who is? Who isn't?
Cooperative Talk	What do you hear the students saying to each other to facilitate engagement? Are they adhering to the social discourse protocols?
Cooperation Signals	Do you see body language indicating frustration? Tuning out? Excitement?
Differing Status	How do high-status students gain or lose in academic and social areas? How do ELs gain or lose in academic, linguistic, and social areas?
Interim and Final Team Products	Is this the level of quality you expected? Does the product meet the content standard? Are students applying academic language? Are they doing close reading and making appropriate interpretations? Are they using academic grammar and appropriate writing conventions?

In addition, figure 2.2 can be used by the students to assess their work in teams.

Factors	4 Always, Excellent Effort	3 Most of the Time, Quite Good Effort	2 Rarely, Effort Was Not Satisfactory
Completed assigned tasks			
Helped other members			
Contributed usefully to group learning			
Made the best use of time during teamwork			

Figure 2.2: Sample rubric for self-assessment and team assessment.

Lesson Delivery

The twelve components of a lesson are intended to be taught sequentially.

1. **Preteaching of vocabulary:** The teacher chooses five or six key words that ELs need to understand to begin to read a passage, guess what is next in the passage, or use in their writing.

2. **Teacher read-alouds and think-alouds:** The teacher models the selected metacognitive strategy.

3. **Student peer reading:** Students read for ten minutes with a peer, alternating sentences and stopping after each paragraph to summarize, clarify information, or pose questions.

4. **Peer summaries:** Peers build joint summaries after each paragraph using tier two and tier three words.

5. **Depth of word studies and grammar:** The teacher demonstrates the parts of speech, a compound sentence, or types of words—such as transition words, polysemous words, cognates, root words, and suffixes—using more sophisticated words or words for specificity.

6. **Class discussions:** The teacher poses a question and prompts a discussion involving all students.

7. **Cooperative learning activities:** Teams of students work together to better learn vocabulary and practice discussion skills.

8. **Bloom-type questions and Numbered Heads Together:** Student teams formulate questions from what they read, and the teacher uses these to test other teams for argumentative practice.

9. **Roundtable reviews:** The teacher facilitates timed round-robin-type writing of tier two and tier three words from memory, oral review of key definitions, and oral review of math or science processes or events in history.

10. **Prewrites and drafting:** The teacher assigns reports, short papers, or research papers.

11. **Revision and editing:** The teacher has students rework pieces such as paragraphs, reports, short papers, long narratives, or research papers.

12. **Final products:** Students present the culmination of their work in the form of a speech, project description, or research presentation.

Depending on the time allocation for a class period, these can be distributed throughout three to five days. Each class period can begin with ten to twelve minutes for teaching new vocabulary words and phrases. Subsequently, more reading with summarization can take place for ten minutes. Otherwise, any of the other components can follow suit, though adhering to the set sequence facilitates student learning. Better learning outcomes result when all of the components are taught.

Here we'll focus on step 1, preteaching of vocabulary. Chapter 3 will focus on steps 2 through 4, and chapter 4 will focus on steps 5 through 12.

Step 1: Preteaching of Vocabulary

Teachers can preteach the vocabulary selected during lesson planning in seven steps (see table 2.2). These seven steps are mainly used for preteaching vocabulary before students read. However, they can also be used to teach words that will be used in a teacher's presentation.

Table 2.2: Seven Steps for Preteaching Vocabulary

Step	Example
1. Teacher says the word or phrase and asks students to repeat it three times.	"Repeat after me, *climate shift*, *climate shift*, *climate shift*."
2. Teacher states the word in context from the text.	"Although many species manage to survive such extreme, long-term *climate shifts*, their living conditions also change."
3. Teacher provides the dictionary definition.	"*Shift* is 'a slight change in position, direction, or tendency.'"
4. Teacher provides the student-friendly definition.	"*Shift* means a change; for instance, the constant *climate shifts* are beginning to worry us."
5. Teacher highlights features of the word: polysemous meanings, cognate, tense, prefixes, and so on.	"*Shift* has multiple meanings. It can be used as a verb to mean to move from one place to another. As a noun, it means a change. It also can mean a time when workers do the same job but at different times, such as the *night shift*, the *morning shift*, or the *afternoon shift*. *Shift* can refer to the part of a car used to change gears. It also is a loosely fitting dress that hangs straight."
6. Teacher engages students in activities to develop word or concept knowledge.	"Turn to your buddy on the right, and take turns saying five or more complete sentences using *climate shifts*, *weather shifts*, *temperature shifts*, and *sea-level shifts*."
7. Teacher reminds students when to use the word.	"Be sure to use *shift* in your partner summaries and in RAFT writing today."

Teachers generally complete steps 1 through 5 in a minute or two. Then, students spend about a minute discussing the vocabulary word with a buddy in step 6. The pair should ping-pong its responses so that students have equal turns and one does not dominate the conversation during the one-minute time frame. This step is critical, since this is the beginning of oracy development. Finally, in step 7, the teacher spends a minute emphasizing how and when to use the word, holding ELs accountable for learning to use it in oral and written discourse.

Some STEM (science, technology, engineering, and mathematics) lessons call for inquiry and labeling of the concepts at the end. This is fine if several other words, particularly tier two words, are pretaught in order for ELs to understand the directions, explanations, and procedures. For instance, key tier three words related to the inquiry can be taught after an experiment or inquiry.

Vocabulary instruction, though recognized as the first of the twelve steps of lesson delivery, is actually utilized throughout the entire learning and teaching process. Consider the following steps that also highlight vocabulary instruction. We will explore each of these steps in depth later in the book.

Class Discussions

At given intervals, five-minute class discussions can take place to debrief to clarify understanding, stress important facts, and consolidate knowledge. After students read sufficient sections of text, the discussions can center on questions that the teacher has prepared in order for students to delve deeper in the text to answer those questions. The teacher poses questions that elicit elaboration and that respond to others' questions and comments. After posing a question, the teacher waits for students to discuss the answer in teams or pairs and then asks for volunteers or calls students at random, including the ELs. He or she directs the discussion and ideas in a way that brings the discussion back on topic as needed. After the students see the teacher model this several times, they can direct their own discussions.

As educators, we must devote time to the subtleties of language use in academic settings. The cultural nuances of oral language and behavior are important to model and teach (Crawford-Brooke, 2013). Teaching students how to ask and respond to questions is crucial, because they will be using them in the reading, information-processing, and writing activities. For instance, students need to learn the subtle differences between:

- "May I ask a question?"
- "Can I ask a question?"
- "I need to ask a question."
- "Are you asking a question or making a statement?"

It is important that students learn the cultural conventions of language needed to participate in group work, cooperative learning activities, and team sports. Taking turns and actively listening are basic skills for academic and social success. Social language skills will help students engage in classroom activities and will help teachers with classroom management issues. Teachers can model various sentence structures when summarizing lessons, dialoguing with students, or asking students for feedback. Consider, for instance, the following sentence structures.

- "The author tells us that . . . What do you think, Linda?"
- "It seems to me that the story is about . . ."
- "As I read the events in the newspaper, I was reminded of . . ."
- "I am not sure that the answer is correct because . . ."
- "If you need a theme for your paper, search . . ."
- "If you want to build the best zoo in your city, which friends from your school would you pick and why? Now, you try asking your question with if . . . then, which . . . and why."

Other sentence and question starters can be glued on a folder to create a table tent. The tents can be placed in areas of the classroom, like desks, where the ELs and other students can readily see them.

Bloom-Type Questions and Numbered Heads Together

After reading a text and going back into that text through peer discussions, the teams can formulate questions using Bloom's Taxonomy question generation charts. (For examples, see in2edu, 2003.) Each team composes two questions and writes each on a separate index card, with the answer on the back. The cards should also contain the name of the team and the level of Bloom's Taxonomy that they used. As students formulate questions, they go back into the text and discuss extensively to create each question. Each question uses key tier two and tier three words and phrases. The teacher collects these cards to use with a cooperative learning strategy called Numbered Heads Together (figure 2.3).

☐ Number off in your team from 1 to 4.
☐ Listen to the question I'm going to ask.
☐ Put your heads together and find the answer in the text.
☐ Make sure everyone in your team knows the answer.
☐ Be prepared to answer when your number is called. I will call these numbers at random.

Figure 2.3: Numbered Heads Together strategy.

Numbered Heads Together serves to hold each student accountable for reading and learning the content of the lesson in order to answer the question. If their number is called, ELs need to be ready to respond for the team by learning phrases or whole sentences. Their peers help them construct these sentences.

The strategy challenges students to go back into the text one more time and delve deeper to answer the question and make sure everyone on the team knows the answer. It becomes a positive competition, as teams try to outperform one another with their questions and with the answers to another team's question.

Depending on the text, this strategy also helps students acknowledge new information expressed by others and, when warranted, modify their own views. With the questions formulated from different levels of Bloom, ELs and all other students get to express facts and opinions that open the discussion with rich elaborations and, if sustained long enough, a variety of points of view. For this stage of a lesson to go well, the teacher can give students sentence starters for agreeing or disagreeing with others politely. (See table 2.3.)

In order to conduct successful argumentative practices, it is also important to preteach how to follow rules for collegial discussions, how to delineate a speaker's argument with specific claims, and the type of attitude one should convey toward the subject or the person speaking. Furthermore, students should have these sentence starters handy for evaluating the soundness of their peers' reasoning and the relevance of their evidence. When one student answers, the next needs to be ready to add a response, contradict, defend a point of view, or substantiate points with evidence.

Interaction During Development of Final Products

In an Expert Jigsaw, another cooperative learning strategy, a text is divided among a team of three or four students. Each student must analyze and master the material in his or her section and present it to the rest of the team, referring to evidence from the text. After each student has presented, the team can probe and reflect on all of the information and ideas to discuss further.

As part of a mini research project, the student teams can then use a graphic organizer to analyze the main ideas and supporting details presented in diverse media and formats (such as visually, quantitatively, and orally) and explain how the ideas clarify the topic, text, or issue under study. Some ELs will have mathematical skills that can be represented quantitatively or in charts, while English-proficient students can interpret in writing or speech. That said, the ELs must also practice explaining the graphic representations with peers and assist in the oral presentation with the small sections they have prepared.

Table 2.3: Sentence Starters for Agreeing and Disagreeing

Context	Sentence Starters
Agree or Acknowledge New Information	"I agree, because . . ." "I concur and would like to add . . ." "I agree, since it says on page . . ." "Along those lines . . ." "I have an example that relates to that . . ." "That is a good place to start . . . "
Disagree	"I disagree with what he said, because . . ." "I understand; however . . ." "On the other hand . . ." "That is a good point or example, but I think . . ." "However, we should remember that . . . "
State an Opinion	"That is a good point, and I believe that . . ." "Along those lines, I would like to add . . ." "The evidence points strongly to . . ." "For example, . . ." "I feel that . . . "
Modify Own Views	"Based on the evidence, I can see how that is a better idea . . ." "I understand the concept now, and . . ." "I can see why now, and . . ." "That makes sense . . ." "I can consider that . . ."
Make Specific Claims	"The evidence for that is on page . . ." "There is still one question to consider . . ." "The evidence I use to support . . . is . . ." "Furthermore, we found these facts . . ." "There is strong evidence to believe that . . ."
Invite Speculation	"I wonder what caused . . ." "Do we want to test . . . to find out if . . ." "I wonder what would happen if . . ." "What do you think will happen next?" "If we change . . . then, would it help?"

In order for students to present claims and findings (such as argument, narrative, and summary presentations) and emphasize salient points in a focused, coherent manner with pertinent facts, details, and examples, the teacher has to be very explicit about the preparation process. Sometimes students are not given sufficient time to prepare and rehearse. Thus, part of the rehearsal, once everything is ready for the formal presentation, should be assistance with delivery skills, such as appropriate eye contact, adequate volume, and clear pronunciation. Teachers can provide ELs with guidance on how to put familiar information together for a presentation by focusing on facts, details, delivery skills, and so on, but they must be very forgiving when it comes to pronunciation. In some cultures, even eye contact has to be overlooked at first but gradually encouraged with time. If students new to the United States are to be college and career ready, we must nurture them and gently guide them toward school success.

Ample time is also necessary for ELs to include multimedia components and visual displays in presentations to clarify findings and claims and emphasize salient points. One middle school in New York City, with a student population that is 90 percent language minority and 40 percent EL, requires even the most limited English proficient students to learn and use PowerPoint and additional information from the Internet. Students are given permission to do their first two or three presentations in their native language, but the rest have to be in English. They learn to adapt a short speech to a variety of contexts and tasks, demonstrating their ongoing command of formal English.

Assessment of Performance

Students need to be assessed frequently during authentic performance; that is, while they are applying new learning, practical application of cognitive skill development, language use, and content understanding can be assessed all at once with simple observation and a checklist or frequent note taking.

Figure 2.4 lists some questions to consider when observing students.

A Cautionary Note About Assessing Vocabulary and Discourse

There are several ways to assess vocabulary for contextual accuracy. However, doing crossword puzzles, defining words, and matching definitions *do not* give a true picture of the students' knowledge of words. Most are guessing games. Instead, real-time use of the words in appropriate contexts will give an accurate picture of students' vocabulary knowledge. Performance assessment is when a teacher can record the use of vocabulary and discourse in real time. For example, when preteaching vocabulary,

Component	Assessment Question
Vocabulary	☐ During the preteaching of vocabulary, does the student give four or five examples of use of a word or phrase to the partner? ☐ Does the student understand the meaning of the word or phrase? ☐ Is the student using the word or phrase correctly? ☐ Does he or she use phrases or complete sentences?
Partner Reading and Summaries	☐ Is the student reading fluently? With prosody? ☐ Are there pronunciation problems? ☐ Are there significant comprehension problems? ☐ Is the student's summary accurate in content? ☐ Is the student using the new vocabulary in the summary?
Class discussions	☐ Is the student participating in the discussion? ☐ How many times? _____ ☐ Are the student's responses and contributions on target in terms of content and his or her language proficiency level?
Writing	☐ Is the student's draft adequate for his or her level of language proficiency and content accuracy? ☐ Is the student's revised version showing improvement on targets for revision? ☐ Does the student's editing focus on target edits? ☐ Does the student need more peer assistance or co-writing with a peer?

Figure 2.4: Questions to consider during student observation.

the teacher can record examples of ways the words learned are used by the students. The ExC-ELL observation protocol and tools help the teacher keep track of and chart student progress. (See appendix F, page 131.) Note taking while watching and listening to students work is also a practical tool for assessing student learning. Another quick way to assess learning at the end of each period is to ask students to use the five words taught at the beginning of the class in a cohesive paragraph, written on an index card or exit pass. Students underline the new words and phrases. It is easy to collect the exit passes as students walk out of class and gauge who did an adequate job using the words and who needs more help.

Table 2.4 (page 42) is a list of activities that students can engage in for teachers to assess student learning and proficiency.

Table 2.4: Activity Assessments

Component	Assessment Options
Vocabulary and Oracy	Participate in a role play. Represent a section of a play, and then role-play the same scene from a different perspective.
	Make a small presentation, or be part of a team presentation on a science experiment or a social studies project.
	Explain a computer game.
	Make a short speech or a newscast.
	Be part of a talk show or a commercial.
	Interview an author.
	Participate in a court case.
Reading and Writing	Create an informational article for a newspaper, writing objectively without personal bias or exposing bias.
	Write an editorial on why a literary piece should receive an award.
	Create an art-based project to compare two characters, literary devices, or historical events.
	Create an architectural design, flyer, or brochure.
	Design a computer game for a mathematics class.
	Create a PowerPoint presentation to illustrate a process.

Summary

Each of the strategies mentioned in this chapter can incorporate the skills specified by content and the English development standards. In the following chapters, we show in detail how interaction skills can be integrated into the remaining steps of lesson delivery.

CHAPTER 3

READING TO LEARN AND LEARNING TO READ

The English learners in your classes might have been sheltered too much! As discussed in the introduction, the curriculum for ELs and low-performing students needs to offer more exposure to a range of texts and tasks than has been done in the past. When they don't read, their vocabularies do not increase. Moreover, ELs are not reading enough. When they do, they pretend to read. They might sound fluent when they read aloud, but they are not getting meaning from the text.

If ELs are to gain adequate access to a range of texts and tasks and the ability to read complex texts in all grades, it is vital that the vocabulary and discourse opportunities in chapter 2 be conducted simultaneously with the complex process of close reading described in this chapter. The Common Core State Standards recommend selecting tier two words and tier three words from passages such as those in appendix A of the CCSS ELA. The following text is from appendix A, and to show the text's complexity, we have bolded the tier three words, italicized the tier two words, and underlined the tier one words.

> In *early times,* no one knew how **volcanoes** *formed* or why they *spouted red-hot* **molten** rock. In *modern times*, scientists began to study **volcanoes**. They <u>still</u> don't know all the answers, but they know much about how a **volcano** works. Our planet is <u>made up</u> of many *layers* of rock. The top *layers* of

solid rock are called the **crust**. Deep <u>beneath</u> the **crust** is the **mantle**, where it is so hot that some rock <u>melts</u>. The melted, or **molten**, rock is called **magma**.

Volcanoes are *formed* when **magma** <u>pushes its way up through the crack</u> in Earth's **crust**. This is called a **volcanic** *eruption*. When **magma** *pours forth* on the *surface*, it is called **lava**. (NGA & CCSSO, 2010b, p. 33)

Thus, this chapter looks at reading instruction for ELs from two angles: (1) comprehending text and (2) analyzing text. In each step of the reading process, there are suggestions for ways to scaffold instruction such as the reading through specialized discourse, sentence frames, additional vocabulary learning at all three tiers, and discussion protocols with suggestions for integrating into each step of the reading process. This approach covers steps 2 through 4 of the lesson delivery framework.

Comprehending Text

All middle and high school teachers are language and reading teachers, right? Years ago when we asked this question, we would get a resounding *no*. Lately, content teachers say, "Yes, but how do I do that?"

The evidence-based reading process for adolescent ELs and low-level readers calls for smaller but meatier pieces of text and quality time to delve into that text for close reading in order to learn the content, learn academic language, and develop advanced reading and critical thinking skills (Calderón, 2012; Coleman & Pimentel, 2012; Short & Fitzsimmons, 2007; Snow & Biancarosa, 2003; Van Lier & Walqui, 2013). Reading is not an end in itself. The way we have tested reading in the past has created fast readers with little comprehension. It is exciting that the Common Core State Standards and the STEM Education Coalition promote literacy as an integral part of science, social studies, math, engineering, and all of the technical fields. After all, depth of comprehension is not only for college-oriented students and ELs. Students interested in becoming beauticians, licensed volunteer nurses, clerical assistants, electricians, or technicians will need to be able to read elaborate instructions, analyze text carefully, and act on these understandings. Ensuring literacy benefits us as well as our students. All students, not just ELs, must have the skills to understand and discuss what they read.

These skills do not happen automatically. Close reading must be explicitly taught in all classrooms and all subjects in middle and high school. Close reading entails identifying key ideas and details, determining craft and structure, and integrating knowledge and ideas as we question the text, understand the author's purpose, and even challenge the messages.

Thomas Newkirk (2010), in "The Case for Slow Reading," describes the need to go back and reread passages several times for deeper and deeper meaning. He also recommends selecting shorter pieces so students can return and find new information, interpretations, or insights. In the case of ELs and low-level readers, this approach helps develop new reading skills and language proficiency as well.

Background knowledge development seems to be a dilemma. The CCSS originally advised against formally prereading texts, but sometimes ELs need background knowledge to comprehend new information. If we do not give sufficient background, how will ELs be able to build new knowledge? But, if we spend too much time giving background knowledge, when will they get to read? This balance is a challenge for teachers with ELs. If a class is going to do a close reading about the Boston Tea Party, for instance, it is important to provide information about the context and even unfamiliar details and key words for ELs, such as what Boston is. However, the teacher mustn't tell the whole story. Some teachers provide summaries in the native language or even in English, defeating the whole purpose for reading.

One way to avoid the pitfall of too much background or preparing for reading is to do the following.

- Preteach five to six key words, mainly tier two words or phrasal clusters. This will help ELs get into the text and begin their reading journey.

- Highlight text features. Charts, graphs, and timelines have important information.

- Highlight text structures and teach the tier two words and phrasal clusters that tend to be used.

- Avoid giving ELs information that will be found in the text or take the place of reading. ELs must read to find information.

Selecting texts to meet the standards is the foundation of close reading, reading comprehension, and mastery of content. However, not all texts are appropriate for close reading. In fact, some longer texts have a lot of fluff, which is why we recommend that teachers parse the text. We use the concept of *parsing* to mean analyzing texts to find important information, lexical complexity, or opportunities to develop comprehension skills that meet the selected standard.

For example, a chapter in a history book might have redundant information—only four pages out of fifteen merit reading. Maybe a complementary two-page article downloaded from the Internet would have additional facts or be better written. Or perhaps a book chapter on biology has important information about living organisms in only five of ten pages, in which case it is better to zoom in on those five pages, and discard the rest. Sometimes teachers are concerned about covering the whole text.

Yet, that doesn't have to happen. It is not breadth but depth. One of the reasons we have administrators attend our professional development sessions with the teachers is for them to understand this and other pedagogical changes that have to be made to support teachers.

Once the text sections and the standards have been selected, the next step is to select words and phrases from all three tiers to preteach before approaching the topic or the text, just as teachers would in the normal lesson delivery process. Key grammatical features or forecasted difficulties can also be highlighted at this point. It's important to keep word and grammar instruction between three and fifteen minutes total at the beginning of the lesson, as students need to get to the reading.

Other materials to have on hand during close reading are the words and standards to be displayed on chart paper, on the SMART Board, on table tents, or as a handout to students. Sentence starters, summary frames, and graphic organizers can be laminated for continuous use, and ancillary materials (such as construction paper, scissors, and sticky notes) can also be used to scaffold the reading and mastery of the content.

The instructional delivery process for developing close reading skills consists of steps 2 through 4 of the lesson delivery framework (see table 3.1).

Table 3.1: The Process for Developing Close Reading Skills

2. **Teacher read-alouds and think-alouds:** The teacher models the selected metacognitive strategy. (3 to 4 minutes)
3. **Student peer reading:** Students read with a peer, alternating sentences and stopping after each paragraph to summarize, clarify information, or pose questions. (10 to 12 minutes)
4. **Peer summaries:** Peers build joint summaries after each paragraph using tier two and tier three words. (10 to 15 minutes)

Although time frames for each activity are given, teachers should adjust the times to fit their classroom schedules. Each of these steps can be planned and mapped out ahead of time by using the lesson planning steps in chapter 2 (page 27). We will discuss each of these steps in detail at the end of this chapter.

Analyzing Text

Most students, including ELs, learned to read with narrative texts: short stories, fables, fiction novels, poetry, and the like. Therefore, when they get to middle and high school, reading expository, informational, or nonfiction texts seems foreign to them. Yet, once they figure out the text features and structures, they become fascinated by the information they can learn about science, geography, history, and current events. For ELs, it is actually much easier to read informational text because they don't have to deal with metaphors, idioms, symbolism, flashbacks, or other literary devices in a language they barely know. As they read about planets or volcanoes or the Boston Tea Party, the redundancy of tier three words and the graphics that usually accompany them become tools for easier comprehension.

Still, reading expository text is quite challenging for ELs, and they need explicit instruction on how to comprehend and analyze those texts. While ELA teachers do teach a combination of narrative and expository reading, this is only one subject the ELs grapple with each day. The majority of their day is spent in courses that require expository text reading skills without also providing the background instruction on building such skills. Content teachers can do so much more for ELs when they preteach the specific words, phrases, text structures, and text features that underscore their discipline. ESL teachers can accelerate learning of English with the same approaches.

Expository texts cover a range of informational and persuasive purposes and text types. There are many types of expository texts: trade books, magazines, newspaper, digital sources, photography essays, and textbooks. The purpose of expository texts is to provide information in different ways, such as the following.

- **Descriptive:** Texts that describe concepts or topics in any subject area

- **Procedural:** How-to texts and manuals, usually written sequentially with visuals

- **Referential:** Mainly reference manuals such as dictionaries and encyclopedias

- **Persuasive:** Argumentative texts such as speeches, editorials, and opinion pieces

- **Comparative:** Usually essays that compare two or more products, books, authors, events, ideas, or characters

However, many texts contain more than one purpose. Therefore, a teacher can peruse a text during lesson preparation to identify the purposes for using that text. For example:

- Is it to simply understand the content being taught?

- Is it to model important comprehension strategies?

- Is it to complement the topic and build background knowledge?

- Is it to understand the text structures of argumentative text?

- Is it a mentor text for writing a comparative essay on a historical event or current event from two sources?

The procedures for teaching reading comprehension to ELs in secondary schools, whether for expository or narrative texts, are basically the same. The same twelve instructional components give ELs the necessary depth and breadth of interaction with language, literacy, and content. While the features of narrative text (plot, dialogue, and setting) differ from those of expository text, they still require close reading and careful analysis to understand narrative craft such as allegory, foreshadowing, and metaphor.

Attributes That Make Text Complex

Narrative text typically has multiple levels of meaning. There are literal and metaphorical meanings. Sometimes, the chronological order is complicated or out of sequence. Narrative texts use flashbacks and foreshadowing. Some texts use more than one voice or point of view. Figurative language such as irony, metaphor, symbolism, idioms, variations of Standard English, and other literary devices make creative texts very difficult for ELs to comprehend.

The CCSS differentiate between the two types of texts by creating separate sets of grade-level standards for each. For instance, consider the seventh grade Reading: Literature standards and Reading: Informational Text standards (table 3.2). Whereas Key Ideas and Details are basically the same for both literature and informational text, the Craft and Structure standards are different.

Table 3.2: The CCSS's Structure for Literature and Informational Text Standards

Domain	Literature Standards	Informational Text Standards
Key Ideas and Details	RL.7.1: Cite several pieces of textual evidence to support analysis of what the text says explicitly as well as inferences drawn from the text.	RI.7.1: Cite several pieces of textual evidence to support analysis of what the text says explicitly as well as inferences drawn from the text.
	RL.7.2: Determine a theme or central idea of a text and analyze its development over the course of the text; provide an objective summary of the text.	RI.7.2: Determine two or more central ideas in a text and analyze their development over the course of the text; provide an objective summary of the text.
	RL.7.3: Analyze how particular elements of a story or drama interact (e.g., how setting shapes the characters or plot).	RI.7.3: Analyze the interactions between individuals, events, and ideas in a text (e.g., how ideas influence individuals or events, or how individuals influence ideas or events).

Craft and Structure	RL.7.4: Determine the meaning of words and phrases as they are used in a text, including figurative and connotative meanings; analyze the impact of rhymes and other repetitions of sounds (e.g., alliteration) on a specific verse or stanza of a poem or section of a story or drama. RL.7.5: Analyze how a drama's or poem's form or structure (e.g., soliloquy, sonnet) contributes to its meaning. RL.7.6: Analyze how an author develops and contrasts the points of view of different characters or narrators in a text.	RI.7.4: Determine the meaning of words and phrases as they are used in a text, including figurative, connotative, and technical meanings; analyze the impact of a specific word choice on meaning and tone. RI.7.5: Analyze the structure an author uses to organize a text, including how the major sections contribute to the whole and to the development of the ideas. RI.7.6: Determine an author's point of view or purpose in a text and analyze how the author distinguishes his or her position from that of others.
Integration of Knowledge and Ideas	RL.7.7: Compare and contrast a written story, drama, or poem to its audio, filmed, staged, or multimedia version, analyzing the effects of techniques unique to each medium (e.g., lighting, sound, color, or camera focus and angles in a film). (RL.7.8 not applicable to literature) RL.7.9: Compare and contrast a fictional portrayal of a time, place, or character and a historical account of the same period as a means of understanding how authors of fiction use or alter history.	RI.7.7: Compare and contrast a text to an audio, video, or multimedia version of the text, analyzing each medium's portrayal of the subject (e.g., how the delivery of a speech affects the impact of the words). RI.7.8: Trace and evaluate the argument and specific claims in a text, assessing whether the reasoning is sound and the evidence is relevant and sufficient to support the claims. RI.7.9: Analyze how two or more authors writing about the same topic shape their presentations of key information by emphasizing different evidence or advancing different interpretations of facts.
Range of Reading and Level of Text Complexity	RL.7.10: By the end of the year, read and comprehend literature, including stories, dramas, and poems, in the grades 6–8 text complexity band proficiently, with scaffolding as needed at the high end of the range.	RI.7.10: By the end of the year, read and comprehend literary nonfiction in the grades 6–8 text complexity band proficiently, with scaffolding as needed at the high end of the range.

Source: NGA & CCSSO, 2010a.

We will use this differentiation to provide a structure and samples for developing curriculum, instruction, and a professional program that addresses the needs of ELs and all their fellow students in their math, science, social studies, and language arts classes. The sample lessons in appendices C, D, and E (page 109, page 115, and page 123) bring all of this together in various content areas.

Text Features and Text Structures

Text features and structures are integral to expository and narrative text. Text features are elements of the external structure, such as tables of contents and illustrations. They are the parts of the text that draw attention to important information and help create meaning. In informational texts, they are like road signs that help readers navigate a reading. Before students read a text, teachers can point out the features the first few times. Thereafter, students should be able to identify and use them as part of their class discussions. The CCSS recommend that students master text features in grades 1 to 3 (NGA & CCSSO, 2010a), but some secondary ELs, especially newcomers, may not understand text features yet.

Text features may fall in the following categories (Fisher, Frey, & Lapp, 2008).

- **Print features:** These guide readers through the organizational pattern; for instance, look at the table of contents, index, glossary, preface, and appendix. Some features, such as tables of contents, are also common to fiction texts.

- **Organizational aids:** These emphasize important information and appear as bold or color print, italics, bullets, titles, headings, subheadings, captions, or sidebars.

- **Graphic aids:** These represent information in a condensed or specific way, such as a diagram, flow chart, sketch, chart, table, cross section, overlay, timeline, figure, or map.

- **Illustrations:** These expand a text's meaning with photos, drawings, and magnifications.

- **Electronic text features:** These expand a text's meaning through hyperlinks, audio buttons, dictionaries, and pronunciation aids.

Text structures, on the other hand, refer to the internal organization of information within a written text. Students learn about text structures as a result of direct instruction. In content classes and throughout their schooling, students must learn to identify various text structures in order to grasp the author's purpose and express the main idea and key points of the passage. The CCSS note the importance of parsing text structures (NGA & CCSSO, 2010a).

> **CCRA.R.5:** Analyze the structure of texts, including how specific sentences, paragraphs, and larger portions of the text (e.g., a section, chapter, scene, or stanza) relate to each other and the whole.

> **RI.11–12.5:** Analyze and evaluate the effectiveness of the structure an author uses in his or her exposition or argument, including whether the structure makes points clear, convincing, and engaging.

In expository texts, authors use text structure to organize and construct ideas or concepts. It is the internal framework that presents and links ideas to meet specific purposes. The author may present ideas and details that can be organized within one or more of the following text structures within paragraphs or across the whole text (Fisher et al., 2008).

- Description
- Cause and effect
- Comparison and contrast
- Sequence or chronology
- Problem and solution
- Enumeration
- Persuasion
- Generalization

Structural elements in narratives differ from expository texts. Narrative elements include the following (Fisher et al., 2008).

- Characters
- Setting
- Plot
- Problem or conflict
- Solution or resolution
- Point of view
- Events
- Theme

Sometimes an author will use different text features and structures within the same text and even within the same paragraph. Therefore, it is critical that students learn that texts often have multiple organizational structures. They must also learn how to identify and connect them across the text. One way a teacher can enhance students' understanding is by using graphic organizers, such as Venn diagrams, webs, timelines, and others to help them visualize a text's internal framework.

Such charts also help students connect thoughts as they practice their discussions around different text structures. Students should keep these charts in their binders or use a laminated copy when discussions begin. It is important for the teacher to teach some of these tier two words about text features and structures through the seven steps for preteaching vocabulary (chapter 2, page 35) and to continuously model how to use them during class discussions. Understanding and recognizing these text elements will help ELs—and all students—better comprehend what they are reading. See appendix A (page 101) for helpful reproducibles on text features and structures.

For both expository and narrative texts, the teacher should first model summarization, which is part of step 2 of the twelve-step lesson delivery framework.

Step 2: Teacher Read-Alouds and Think-Alouds

The teacher selects a section of text and reads each sentence aloud, pausing frequently to clarify meaning or to ponder and ask questions about the sentence content. After one or two sentences, the teacher says aloud what he or she understands about each sentence. Consider this teacher who reads a passage on migration. Her response might be something like the following; notice that she makes sure to introduce the concept of summarization at the outset.

> *Summarizing is something we do all the time! If we tell a friend what the movie was about or what we did during summer vacation, we don't tell him or her everything that happened. That would take too long and be too much information. Instead, we tell the general idea and include the most important points. In other words, we summarize and tell the key points or sum it up. When we summarize, we create a short version of the information and include the essential information in the same order as the original, and we try to use as many tier two and tier three words as possible. For example, this paragraph says:*

> Human migration is the movement of humans from one place to another, sometimes over long distances or in large groups. Human migration has been taking place as long as humans have lived on Earth. More recently, migration was the reason that the population of what is now called the United States changed dramatically during the 1600s and 1700s, when colonists from England (Britain) settled in specific parts of the country, often on land that had been occupied by Native Americans.

> *I'm going to break this paragraph down and then summarize what I read.* Migration is a natural part of our lives—*the author is talking about* migration, *which is another word for* movement. *The author says that this is part of our lives. I guess she must mean that it is a part of all of our lives. Let's see if that's true—*Birds migrate with changes in the weather, and we might be accustomed to seeing a particular type of bird (like geese) at one time of the year and not another, or we see geese flying in flocks overhead as they migrate to the south or to the north, depending on the time of year.

> *This is a long sentence. Let's see if I can break it up. She is saying that birds migrate, or move, when the weather changes, and she mentions geese specifically. She says that geese migrate at certain times of the year and that they fly north or south.* Not only birds, but also fish, butterflies, insects, and even plants migrate—*so it looks like everything that lives migrates. And finally, humans migrate, which is the focus of this article.*

I'm going to summarize this paragraph using tier two and tier three words. This paragraph tells me that humans have been migrating for a long time. Between the years 1600 and 1700, colonists from England migrated and settled in America. They usually settled on lands that Native Americans occupied.

Teachers usually make use of read-alouds and think-alouds to help students learn how to summarize. As noted earlier, students must learn how to identify text structure in their readings in order to grasp the author's purpose and express the main idea and key points of the passage in their summaries. These summaries indicate the degree of understanding and learning that result from reading. Therefore, they also serve as an effective assessment tool. Teachers can use the rubric in figure 2.2 (page 33) to record these data.

Step 3: Student Peer Reading

After preteaching key terminology and modeling a comprehension strategy, ELs can begin to read the text with a peer. Peer reading has been found to be the best approach to delve into close reading for ELs (Calderón, Slavin, & Sánchez, 2011; Shanahan, 2012; Slavin & Madden, 2001). Peer reading for ELs and low-level readers and students with low comprehension skills consists of reading aloud with a partner alternating sentences. Templates for concept mapping, note-taking strategies, and quick summaries can accompany peer reading. There are variations to the strategy, but the most basic and effective process for ELs requires the following five steps, which should last about ten minutes.

1. The teacher reads and models strategies for analyzing text.

2. Partner A reads the first sentence. Partner B helps if necessary.

3. Partner B reads the next sentence. Partner A helps if necessary.

4. After each paragraph, the partners collaborate to summarize orally what they have just read, using many of the tier two and three words or both, and do a think-aloud.

5. Partners continue until they finish reading the section assigned.

Teachers should pair ELs with friendly students who are more advanced readers. Although the reading is done in pairs, students typically sit in heterogeneous teams of four to allow for the other reading strategies. This facilitates all of the team activities that follow peer reading and makes it easier for the teacher to monitor and record learning progressions. Can you imagine the effect on ELs when they work with partners and teams in all their core content classrooms?

After ten or so minutes of peer reading, the teacher can have a class discussion on the content just read, use choral reading in which teams or the whole class read in unison, teach more words before students continue reading the next sections, or ask students to do silent reading with peer summaries after each paragraph or page.

Silent Reading With Peer Summary

Silent reading alone has proven ineffective for most low-level readers and ELs (Calderón, 2007; Shanahan, 2012). When ELs read silently, there is no way for the teacher to know if they understand what they are reading. There is neither peer assistance nor clarification of vocabulary or concepts. If a teacher has not pretaught key vocabulary, she can never be sure that students will comprehend. Comprehension improves when students read one or two paragraphs silently and then discuss the content with a peer. Peer discussions should be frequent, occurring at least every five minutes or so. The more complex the text, the shorter the chunks that students should read silently before meeting with a partner for peer discussion and summarization using as many tier two and three words as possible.

ELs should not be told to summarize in their own words. Their discourse will not improve if they are not held accountable for using at least three to five new words each time they summarize. Effective teachers mill around monitoring on-task behavior and taking notes on how students conduct their summaries, if they use tier two and three words, and if they understand the text. Teachers can record this type of performance assessment for sets of students and store it in student portfolios electronically or on paper.

Triads and Shadow Reading

When a newcomer arrives, he or she can be placed in a pair of students who already work effectively and are willing to take in a newcomer. At first, the newcomer sits in the middle of two partners and only listens as they read alternating sentences. Sometimes he or she tracks while each peer is reading and the peer not reading monitors the tracking.

After a week or two, the newcomer begins to shadow read as part of that triad. Shadow reading is when the newcomer reads at a low whisper with each partner. When ready and confident, the newcomer reads a complete sentence, receiving help if necessary. Still sitting in the middle of the triad, he or she will get twice as many turns as students alternate sentences.

Reciprocal Teaching

The peer-reading routine *reciprocal teaching* (Palincsar & Brown, 1984) has been very effective with ELs and other students. Students in groups of four read small sections silently and then stop to summarize and clarify or teach each other, as in previous strategies, but in reciprocal teaching, each student also assumes a role: summarizer, questioner, clarifier, or connector. The summarizer highlights key ideas up to the point of reading; the questioner poses questions about unclear parts, puzzling information, connections to other concepts, and the big picture; the clarifier addresses confusing parts and attempts to answer the team's questions; and the connector suggests how certain themes and concepts connect to other texts, theories, processes, or solutions.

Students read silently for about ten minutes or so and then begin discussing from these four roles. We've modified the roles and discourse in table 3.3 to coincide with the CCSS for grades 9–12.

Table 3.3: Reciprocal Teaching Roles and Sentence Starters

Role	Sentence Starters
Summarizer	"This section is mostly about . . ." "The main idea is . . ." "The topic sentence is . . ." "Some details are . . ." "One argument might be . . ."
Questioner	"Why is . . . significant?" "Why does . . . happen?" "How is . . . an example of . . . ?" "What is the most important . . . ?" "What can we predict for the next section?" "Why are those words repeated in the poem?"
Clarifier	"What do we need to clarify?" "Which word or phrase?" "A part we don't understand?" "Why is the author saying . . . ?"
Connector	"How is this similar to . . . ?" "Let's compare this to . . ." "Why is it different from . . . ? "What do . . . and . . . have in common?" "What evidence do we have for that?" "How does that compare to today's problems?"

Reciprocal teaching is more effective for ELs at higher levels of language and literacy (levels 5 to 6), whereas partner reading is best for students at beginning, intermediate, and advanced levels (levels 1 to 6). Partner reading and reciprocal teaching can be combined for levels 3 to 6.

Step 4: Peer Summaries

A team of four can quickly summarize information the teacher presents, such as a mathematics problem or a science experiment. The teacher pauses at key intervals and asks students to quickly summarize the information in teams round-robin style. Each student must use a different sentence starter to contribute one important piece of information, such as:

- "Initially, the teacher said . . ."
- "Following that . . ."
- "Subsequently . . ."
- "Finally . . ."

Once students have practiced summarizing in pairs and teams, the teacher models how to summarize a paragraph or brief passage by answering the questions in figure 3.1. Students use the information to generate an oral summary and then a written summary. Teachers can even use the written summaries as exit passes to assess student language and knowledge.

Narrative	Expository
1. Who or what is this about?	1. Who or what is this about?
2. What was the most important thing that happened?	2. What was the most important information presented?
Example: There were three main characters. The first one was rich. The second was smart. The third loved life.	**Example:** The atmosphere is the layer of the gases that surrounds the Earth. It makes life on Earth possible.

Figure 3.1: Summary prompts for narrative and expository texts.

As students engage with more extensive text, they can also use the summarizing techniques in figure 3.2. The narrative strategy helps students use plot and resolution to identify important elements. The expository summary, which is similar to a reporter's approach, helps students identify important facts.

A close look at the responses to the expository strategy shows that as the reader answers the questions, she notices that the main idea reveals a cause-and-effect text structure. In addition, she uses the word *cause* in three of the responses. Higher levels can synthesize the information gleaned from the prompt and consolidate it. Figure 3.3 includes summary templates for both expository and narrative texts. In addition, the summary rubric in appendix B (page 107) can help students self-assess their summary skills.

Narrative Strategy	Expository Strategy
Somebody (character)	**What or who** is this mostly about? Subject or topic?
Wanted (character's goal)	**What** is most important about this subject or topic?
But (conflict facing character)	**Where** did this occur?
So (how character reacts to conflict)	**Why** is the subject or topic important?
Then (resolution of the conflict)	**How** did this occur?
Student Example (EL levels 1 and 2): The Big Bad Wolf wanted to eat the pigs for dinner, but they hid in the brick house. So, the wolf went hungry. Then, the pigs celebrated.	**Connectors: consequently, additionally, thus**
	Student Example (EL levels 1 and 2):
	What—Rising sea levels
	What—World temperature causes sea levels to rise or fall.
Student Example (EL levels 3 and 4): Diana Nyad wanted to swim from Cuba to Florida since 1978, but weather and physical limits stifled her dream. So she kept training and trying to "find a way." Then, on September 2, 2013, she became the first to swim from Cuba to Florida without a protective cage.	**Where**—Coastal areas, river deltas
	Why—Melting glaciers will cause flooding.
	How—The warming of the polar regions causes ice to melt and seas to rise.
	Student Example (EL levels 3 and 4): A warming world results in rising sea levels. As world temperatures rise, glaciers around the world melt. Consequently, coastal areas and river deltas will be flooded, and some land will disappear.

Source: Adapted from Austin Independent School District, n.d.

Figure 3.2: Sample summary strategies for narrative and expository texts.

Expository and Nonfiction Cues	Our Summary
Connectors: consequently, additionally, thus	
What/Who is this mostly about? Subject or topic?	
What is most important about this subject or topic?	
Where did this occur?	
Why is the subject or topic important?	
How did this occur?	

Figure 3.3: Expository and narrative summary templates. continued >

Narrative and Literary Cues	Our Summary
Somebody (character)	
Wanted (character's goal)	
But (conflict facing character)	
So (how character reacts to conflict)	
Then (resolution of the conflict)	

Text-Based Discourse

In the workplace, communication skills are key to success. These often include reading and processing information as well as summarizing information orally or in the form of reports or electronic documents. These are essential skills for social workers, health care professionals, scientists, engineers, data analysts, and a multitude of other professions.

Teachers can use text-based questions and questions at higher levels of Bloom's Taxonomy to direct students to identify the main idea of a passage and the author's craft. Such questions call attention to key words that serve as signals for different text structures. As noted earlier, sometimes an author will use different text structures within the same text and even within the same paragraph. Therefore, it is critical that students learn that texts can have multiple organizational structures; they must be able to identify and connect them across a text. In either case, the teacher can enhance students' understanding by helping them visualize a text's internal framework by using graphic organizers, such as Venn diagrams, webs, timelines, and so on.

Summarizing different types of texts exposes ELs to hard or important words and encourages them to zoom in on precise meanings. Figure 3.4 helps students connect thoughts as they practice their discussions around different text structures. It should be given to the students to keep in their binders or laminated for students to keep handy when discussions begin. It is important for the teacher to teach some of these tier two words through the seven steps (chapter 2, page 35) and to continuously model how to use them during class discussions.

In some cases, especially when students' English development is in the early stages, it is also helpful to use paragraph frames related to the dominant internal structure of the text and highlight the corresponding signal words and transition words that help ideas flow. (See figure 3.5.)

Students need to know what the text reveals about the author's purpose and how the author uses key words to organize the flow and relationship among ideas. Thus, these tools help students sort information and create an effective summary, which are powerful learning strategies.

Major evidence or details in support:	Significant responses to counterclaims:

Conclusion:

Figure 3.4: Sample graphic organizer for viewpoints or claims.

Problem-Solution Paragraph Frame

"_____ had, was, or is a problem, because _____ . Therefore, _____ . As a result, _____ ."

Compare-and-Contrast Paragraph Frame

"_____ and _____ are alike but also different in several ways. First, they are alike because _____ . However, they are different because _____ . Additionally, _____ is _____ while _____ is _____ . Finally, _____ and _____ are mostly _____ ."

Sources: Achievement Strategies, n.d.; Orcutt, n.d.

Figure 3.5: Sample paragraph frames.

Magnet Summaries

Another technique for teaching summaries is the Magnet Summary (Meade PASS Training, n.d.), which uses key vocabulary as a jumping-off point. Just as a magnet attracts metal, key vocabulary or magnet words can attract information about a topic. Magnet words tend to be tier three words but can also include tier two vocabulary. They are often used in titles and headings, embedded in the text, or included in text features such as captions and sidebars.

After watching a teacher model the strategy with a brief text, a student locates the key words and phrases related to the given text's topic. She then writes each magnet word or phrase in the center of an index card. Next, she identifies details from the text to support the magnet term and writes these around the term. Finally, on the back of the index card, she writes a summary using the magnet term and the supporting details (see figure 3.6). The goal is to write a one- or two-sentence summary.

Teachers can also use this strategy to generate oral summaries during peer reading. After reading a paragraph or assigned section, students collaborate, underline or list the magnet words or phrases along with supporting details, and then work together to generate an oral summary. Students can also generate Magnet Summaries on designated topics as a consolidation activity at the end of class (Meade PASS Training, n.d.) by underlining the tier two and tier three words that the teacher has previously taught.

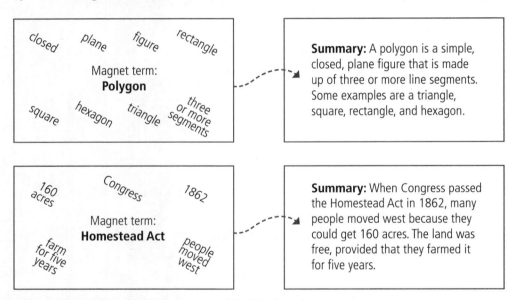

Source: Adapted from Frederick County Public Schools, n.d.

Figure 3.6: Sample Magnet Summaries.

Summarization as the Cornerstone of Comprehension

Summarizing is, perhaps, the most common and most necessary strategy. It requires that the student provide a general recitation of the key text content (Allington, 2001). Learning to summarize helps students add information to the stores of knowledge organized in their brains. It also helps them take information from the text and make it their own (Fountas & Pinnell, 2001).

Summarizing can be done in writing, but also orally, dramatically, artistically, visually, physically, musically, in groups, or individually. Summarization is one of the most underused teaching techniques we have today, yet research has shown that it yields some of the greatest leaps in comprehension and long-term retention of information (Wormeli, 2005).

Robert Marzano (2010) states that just as comprehension is a cherished skill in language arts, it is also critical to understanding texts in general; furthermore, "comprehension is based on summarizing—restating content in a succinct manner that highlights the most crucial information." Consequently, the process of summarization requires more instructional attention, particularly with ELs.

Summarization requires that the reader identify key information. To determine what information to present in a narrative text summary, the reader must first identify what internal text structure the author utilized. Awareness of the text structure helps readers align their thinking with that of the author and promotes comprehension.

Narrative text often uses the structure known as story grammar, which comprises the literary elements of characters, setting, problem and solution, and plot. A narrative develops real or imagined events with effective literary techniques, relevant descriptive details, and event sequences. It also usually includes a conclusion that follows from and reflects on the narrated experiences or events. In contrast, expository text uses a variety of organizational frameworks to present ideas and information depending on the author's purpose. An expository text conveys ideas, concepts, and information within an appropriate organizational structure. It utilizes precise language and domain-specific vocabulary. It often includes a concluding statement or section that supports the information or explanation presented (Calderón, Carreón, Cantú, & Minaya-Rowe, 2012). Therefore, when the passage is a narrative, the goal is to summarize important information related to the plot. If the passage is expository, the goal is to summarize information important to the topic.

Local, district, state, and national U.S. standards require students to know how to summarize. For example, in the CCSS, formal summarization typically begins in grade 4 with the main idea and continues to grade 12, when students summarize in a more sophisticated way (NGA & CCSSO, 2010a); consider the following standards for reading.

> **RI.4.2:** Determine the main idea of a text and explain how it is supported by key details; summarize the text.

> **RI.11–12.2:** Determine two or more central ideas of a text and analyze their development over the course of the text, including how they interact and build on one another to provide a complex analysis; provide an objective summary of the text.

Summarization benefits students and teachers (see table 3.4). It also helps the teacher gather performance data on students. The teacher can listen to the peer summaries as he or she walks around the classroom with a checklist or an observation protocol like the one in appendix F (page 131).

Table 3.4: Benefits of Summarization

Benefits for Students	Benefits for Teachers
Provides an opportunity to identify and verbalize what is important	Provides evidence of the student's ability to select important information
Serves as a means to check comprehension	Serves as an informal indicator of comprehension
Provides practice in decision making and sequencing	Reveals a student's ability to prioritize and sequence
Promotes the development of academic language	Provides evidence of student's language development
Provides an opportunity to identify an author's purpose and related text structure	Indicates understanding of text structure and its use in a student's writing
Engages the student in analyzing, synthesizing, and consolidating information	Demonstrates a student's ability to use critical-thinking skills
Promotes learning and retention	Provides evidence of student learning

Source: Adapted from Maryland Public Television, 2013.

Summary

Teaching students to generate oral or written summaries using the appropriate technique to meet the lesson's goals is an effective and efficient approach for improving comprehension and retention, developing academic vocabulary and oral or written discourse, and building critical-thinking skills that will prepare students for the college and future careers. Teachers can even give extra credit when students accurately use tier two and three words and phrases.

The next chapter continues with the reading process by addressing depth of word learning, grammar, and additional discourse for class discussions, collaborative student work, and instructional strategies for delving deeper into the text and to anchor language, literacy, and content.

CHAPTER 4

ANCHORING LANGUAGE, LITERACY, AND CONTENT AFTER READING

Close reading of expository and narrative text means returning several times to develop students' ability to comprehend and work with complex text. We've covered the first four steps of the twelve-step process in chapters 2 and 3. We'll continue here with steps 5 through 9 (table 4.1, page 64).

Step 5: Depth of Word Studies and Grammar

In this chapter, *grammar* refers to the structures and features of language, particularly the structure and arrangement of words in phrases and sentences (syntax) within written discourse. Understanding grammar and syntax helps students perform basic language tasks such as analyzing paragraphs sentence by sentence and word by word to determine the role these sentences and words play in a paragraph and overall text. When a student is unfamiliar with the grammar and syntax of English—which are closely related—it is difficult for him or her to determine meaning, especially when symbols, key terms, and other domain-specific words and phrases are involved. Beyond the literal meaning of words on a page, grammar and syntax also help students analyze the author's purpose in providing an explanation, describing procedure, or discussing an experiment in a text. Thus, these building blocks of language are also the building blocks of understanding for ELs and all students. Unfortunately, many secondary ELs either didn't

Table 4.1: The Process for Teaching Comprehension of Complex Text

5. **Depth of word studies and grammar:** The teacher demonstrates the parts of speech, a compound sentence, or types of words—such as transition, polysemous, cognates, root words, and suffixes—using more sophisticated words or words for specificity.

6. **Class discussions:** The teacher poses a question and prompts a discussion involving all students.

7. **Cooperative learning activities:** Teams of students work together to better learn vocabulary and practice discussion skills.

8. **Bloom-type questions and Numbered Heads Together:** Student teams formulate questions from what they read, and the teacher uses these to test other teams for argumentative practice.

9. **Roundtable reviews:** The teacher facilitates timed round-robin-type writing of tier two and tier three words from memory, oral review of key definitions, and oral review of math or science processes or events in history.

receive this instruction or were moved through the grade levels regardless of understanding, so secondary teachers need to ensure these building blocks are in place prior to moving forward with literacy in various content areas.

Some of the more common issues ELs have with grammar and syntax include the following. Teachers should be on the lookout for red flags and address these issues as early as possible.

- **Compound and complex sentences:** Within a sentence, information is presented in a series of clauses, each containing a different idea or message. A clause contains a subject and a verb (denoting an event, action, activity, or state). An independent clause—"genes contain instructions for assembling amino acids into proteins"—can stand alone as a complete sentence. A dependent clause—"when Mendel took charge of the monastery garden"—cannot stand alone.

- **Nominalization and long noun phrases:** Nominalization refers to the use of a verb or adjective as a noun or noun phrase. For example, *germination* is a noun derived from the verb *germinate*. Some examples of sentences using nominalization or long noun phrases include "*Ecosystem destabilization* can occur when the climate changes rapidly" or "An *indication* of climate change's effect is the migration of both animals and plants."

Other word families include the following (table 4.2).

Table 4.2: Word Families

Noun	Verb	Adverb	Adjective
Assumption	Assume	Assumedly	Assuming
Protection	Protect	Protectively	Protective
Attraction	Attract	Attractively	Attractive
Development	Develop	Developmentally	Developmental
Relation	Relate	Relationally	Relative

- **Passive voice structures:** Verbs can be either active or passive. When active, the subject completes the action the verb intends. When passive, it's not always clear who or what completes the action. Thus, passive voice is generally frowned upon as it is not as clear. Consider the difference between "Many enzymes are affected by changes in temperature" and "Changes in temperature affect many enzymes."

  Other examples include the following:

  - Cells are surrounded by a barrier called a cell membrane.
  - These cellular properties cannot be measured.
  - Its origins had been almost forgotten.
  - Many seeds are eaten or hidden by small animals.
  - Fresh water can get polluted as it runs off.
  - Pollen is produced by stamens.

- **Prepositional phrases and idioms:** A *prepositional phrase* is a preposition that precedes a noun phrase. Typically, academic text contains several prepositional phrases within a complex sentence, which can be confusing for ELs. For example, "The energy stored by producers can be passed through an ecosystem along a food chain, a series of steps in which organisms transfer energy by eating and being eaten." Common prepositional phrases include *according to, aside from, because of,* and *such as.* An *idiom* is a term or phrase whose meaning is independent from the literal definitions of its parts. Instead, it refers to a figurative meaning that is known only through common use. An idiom is generally a colloquial metaphor, a term that requires some foundational knowledge, information, or experience, to use only within a culture where parties have common reference. Common idiomatic phrases include *on account of, the bottom line, on the cutting edge,* and *state of the art.*

Students must be familiar with such words and phrasings not only to be successful in classrooms but also to be successful on standardized tests. Here are the most frequent tier two words and phrasal clusters that can be found in some state exams:

- Accuracy
- Additive
- Affect
- Allow
- Apparent
- Apparently
- Approach
- Arrange
- Assortment
- Assumption
- Bases
- Basis
- Behavior

- Belief
- Body
- Boundary
- Core
- Criteria
- Crucial
- Depict
- Deplete
- Device
- Display
- Distinct
- Effect
- Generate

- Illustrate
- Impact
- In the absence of . . .
- Conclusion that can be drawn . . .
- Damage to which will most directly . . .
- Most closely resembles . . . this is due to . . .
- Which procedure would most likely . . .

Here is a little exercise. In figure 4.1, identify the words or clauses an EL might have difficulties with.

A growing number of studies suggest, however, that such an increase could have a big impact on life and we would all kick the bucket.

As a result of his fruitful efforts on behalf of specific community members, he was given a blank check by the chief stakeholders regarding the next steps to be taken for the sake of the community as a whole.

Figure 4.1: Sample complex text.

When students are explicitly taught grammar and syntax, they are better able to note and assess patterns of writing and what they achieve, and they can use words, phrases, and clauses to create cohesion and clarify the relationships among claims, counterclaims, reasons, and evidence. Not only can they understand the meaning of another writer, but they can also create meaning themselves!

Step 6: Class Discussions

Summarizing or paraphrasing is very important for ELs to master, but it is still pretty low on Bloom's continuum of lower- to higher-order thinking. If students cannot summarize the basic content of a passage and learn to use precise words and phrases in their summaries, it will be almost impossible to analyze the fine points of content.

The teacher can model posing and answering questions that will lead students to make appropriate inferences about what the author is trying to show. A class discussion can be conducted with the teacher asking questions such as the ones below. Then, gradually the teacher can release the responsibility to teams of students to practice similar questions with another section of the text. Finally, individual students can work on such questions with the remainder of the text. It is important that individual work be checked with peers for confirmation and more learning.

The standards strongly focus on students gathering evidence, knowledge, and insight from what they read and therefore require that a majority of the questions and tasks that students ask and respond to be based on the text under consideration (Coleman & Pimentel, 2012). The questions that teachers ask should require students to demonstrate that they can follow the details in a text and make valid claims that stem from evidence in a text. High-quality, text-dependent questions should engage students to attend to the particular dimensions, ideas, and specifics of that text. Each text will generate different questions. The questions should be aligned to the standards—not just to the content standards but also to the language proficiency standards. This is where the integration of language, literacy, and content occurs.

Questions for expository text should focus on analyzing the arguments and information. They should provide students with sufficient evidence to be ready to write cohesive pieces to inform or explain the content they read closely and discussed through peer and whole-class discussions. Questions for narrative text should also focus on the information students are to learn and discover in a text and the author's purpose, consider other sources to compare and contrast, and challenge the messages.

High-quality, text-dependent questions help students attend to the particular dimensions, ideas, and specifics of that text. In addition to learning academic language and thinking critically, students who formulate strong questions delve deeper and deeper in the text to come up with questions to challenge each other. They like the competitive nature of the task. Questions that students can answer without looking at the text—such as "Why did your parents migrate to the United States?" or "What country would you like to go to?"—are simply distractions. Although these types of questions might appeal to ELs and get them talking, they will not move ELs closer to understanding the text. Rather, the goal of formulating questions is to help students learn to:

- Ask and answer questions that they can only answer by referring explicitly back to the text

- Go back into the text and see something they would not have seen before

- Extract key meanings or ideas from the text

Here are some steps for writing questions for close analytic reading.

1. After selecting key vocabulary to preteach, go back and identify those tier one, two, and three words and phrases that will support deeper reading comprehension.

2. Look for those sentences that contain the elements listed in the previous section (such as phrasal clusters, compound sentences, and passive voice).

3. Revisit the standards you selected and see if there are other sentences worthy of analyzing.

4. Find sections that will create difficulties for the ELs and craft questions that will support the ELs in mastering those sections. Areas requiring inferences will be some of the most difficult.

5. Create three or four text-dependent questions for each section that the students will be reading. Write your expected answer along with your question.

6. Assess your questions by noting student responses. Assess their knowledge of the language and content by their answers. Assess transfer into their skill by having them formulate questions in teams and, later, independently. Also test them through strategies such as Numbered Heads Together.

Each type of text will, of course, generate different questions. Questions for expository text should focus on analyzing the arguments and information, such as the following.

- What does the author want me to understand in this passage?

- Who is speaking in the passage?

- Who seems to be the main audience?

- What is the most important point here? Why?

- What's another important thing?

- What does the author mean by _____ ?

- What are some words or phrases I don't understand?
  - What is the main idea?
  - Is there a message in the main idea?
  - What are some interesting passages? Why?

Questions for narrative text, on the other hand, should focus on the author's purpose. Consider these examples.

- Why did the author choose those symbols?
- What is being compared?
- Do I find any metaphors? Similes? Personification?
- What words seem important? Why?
- What types of words is the text using?
- What words, phrases, or sentences do I not understand?
- Why is the author using incomplete sentences?
- What tone does the text use?

Step 7: Cooperative Learning Activities

As discussed in chapter 1 in the context of classroom structures, cooperative learning activities are an excellent way to help all students interact while also learning vocabulary and practicing discussion skills. The Common Core State Standards clearly rely on a cooperative learning classroom context to facilitate ample interaction and development of academic language. The CCSS clearly facilitate student interaction with and development of academic language. For instance, the grade 7 standards for Speaking and Listening state that students should (NGA & CCSSO, 2010a) do the following.

> **SL.7.1:** Engage effectively in a range of collaborative discussions (one-on-one, in groups, and teacher led) with diverse partners on grade 7 topics, texts, and issues, building on others' ideas and expressing their own clearly.

> **SL.7.1.B:** Follow rules for collegial discussions, track progress toward specific goals and deadlines, and define individual roles as needed.

> **SL.7.1.C:** Pose questions that elicit elaboration and respond to others' questions and comments with relevant observations and ideas that bring the discussion back on topic as needed.

> **SL.7.1.D:** Acknowledge new information expressed by others and, when warranted, modify their own views.

To incorporate cooperative learning strategies into the classroom, teachers must ensure that students are assigned tasks as opposed to roles (such as time keeper, writer, reporter, leader, and so on) to perform with their peers. For instance, sometimes peers assign meaningless roles to ELs, such as drawing or keeping time. If students are assigned tasks, however, their proficiency will stretch and their team will hold them accountable for using new vocabulary. Roles limit students in their participation in learning the targeted academic knowledge and cooperative learning skills, while tasks prevent students from freeloading during the activities and ensure that they fully participate. Essentially, tasks help create a collective responsibility for the group's success and individual opportunity for self-expression and reflection (Calderón et al., 2015).

As teachers facilitate these strategies, they must have both homogeneous and heterogeneous groupings. They must also consolidate or anchor content knowledge so that all or most students know the content and use the correct terms and proper grammar. They need to understand what students know, what connections are still missing, and what they need to include in future classes. It's also important to assess and address all students' unique needs, including ELs and those who are reluctant to participate.

See appendix B (page 107) for a summary rubric students can use to self-assess during cooperative learning summaries and discussions.

Step 8: Bloom-Type Questions and Numbered Heads Together

Chapter 2 describes the process for formulating questions using Bloom's Taxonomy and the Numbered Heads Together strategy to motivate the students to write quality questions for competing with other class teams. So why should students formulate questions around the text they are reading instead of just answering questions? In addition to learning the proper language for question formulation at different levels of critical thinking, the students must go back into the text to delve deeper in order to come up with questions that will test the other teams' knowledge of that text. They like that challenge, and they like the competitive nature of the task.

Before having students formulate their questions, teachers should use the following criteria to properly model question formulation.

- Write questions that can only be answered by referring explicitly back to the text being read.

- Make sure your questions have students going back into the text to see something they would not have seen before.

- Help students extract key meanings or ideas found in the text.

- Help students analyze a complex sentence or an inference or the strategy you have been practicing with this text.

Once the teacher has modeled question formulation, he or she can teach how to formulate questions for the six levels of Bloom's Taxonomy. Here are sample prompts for level 5 (analysis).

- What is the function of . . . ?
- What's fact? Opinion?
- What assumptions . . . ?
- What statement is relevant?
- What motive is there?
- Related to, extraneous to, not applicable.
- What conclusions . . . ?
- What does the author believe?
- What does the author assume?
- Make a distinction.
- State the point of view of . . .
- What is the premise?
- What ideas apply?
- What ideas justify the conclusion?
- What's the relationship between . . . ?
- The least essential statements are . . .
- What's the main idea? Theme?
- What inconsistencies or fallacies exist?
- What literary form is used?
- What persuasive technique . . . ?
- Implicit in the statement is . . .

When student team members reach consensus on their Bloom-type questions, they write them on an index card, with the expected answers on the back. The teacher collects them and transitions into Numbered Heads Together. The teacher selects one question, reads it, and asks the students to put their heads together, go back into the text, find the answer, discuss, and make sure everyone is ready to answer if his or her number is called. All students with that number stand when the number is called.

Depending on the text, this strategy also helps students acknowledge new information that others express and, when warranted, modify their own views. For this stage of a lesson to go well, the teacher can give students sentence starters for agreeing or disagreeing with others politely. (See table 4.3, page 72.)

Once the students are comfortable with level 1 (knowledge), they move on to level 2 (understanding), and subsequently to all six levels. When newcomers arrive in the middle of the year, they can practice formulating questions beginning with level 1, even though the other students might be working with higher levels.

As with any cooperative learning strategy, the teacher sets the expectations and monitors the work in teams. By collecting a few samples of questions being drafted, the teacher might find that a minilesson on question formulation might be necessary. Even though the Bloom charts have many examples of model question starters, students often get confused with the different levels.

Table 4.3: Sentence Starters for Agreeing and Disagreeing

Context	Sentence Starters
Agreeing	"I agree, because . . ." "I concur and would like to add . . ." "I agree, since it says on page . . ." "Along those lines . . ." "I have an example that relates to that . . ." "That is a good place to start . . . "
Disagreeing	"I disagree with what he said, because . . ." "I understand; however . . ." "On the other hand . . ." "That is a good point or example, but I think . . ." "However, we should remember that . . . "

Step 9: Roundtable Reviews

Roundtable reviews can be used to see how many words students remember. Basically, it helps students become more accountable for remembering words. It is also a good way to learn to spell the words. Students like the healthy competition between teams, since the team with the greatest number of words is recognized, as is the team with the greatest improvement score on the second round. The teams are heterogeneous in order to create as much equity as possible for each team.

Roundtable review consists of two stages and an intermission. In stage 1, which is allotted two minutes, students follow these five steps.

1. Clear your desks.

2. Use only one paper and pencil for the group.

3. One student in each group writes a tier two or three word or phrase from memory from the text the class has been reading and passes the paper to the right.

4. The next student does the same.

5. Keep writing one word or phrase at a time until the teacher calls time.

Teams then count and report the number of responses and receive a team score based on the number of terms they were able to write down in one minute.

Next begins the intermission, during which students delete repeated words and correct spelling, and they report their corrected number and read the list to the class. The teacher then interviews the team with the most words and asks students to share their strategy. As a response, all teams take four minutes to go back into the text and come up with a strategy for improving their score the second time.

At this point, stage 2 begins. It follows the same rules as stage 1, and teams use a clean sheet of paper. To close, the class debriefs. How many teams improved their scores? What helped them improve? What else did students learn? Students like the healthy competition between teams, since the team with the greatest number of words gets recognition, as does the team with the greatest improvement score on the second round.

Teachers typically find that all teams improve during the second round. The intermission serves an important impetus in this change; it is an opportunity for self-improvement and team interdependence, in addition to reviewing vocabulary and going back into the text. This is a second chance to bring up more words that lie dormant. Approaching rereading during the intermission is particularly important for ELs. They welcome the opportunity to go back into the text and make a greater effort to learn more words. ELs also benefit from the interaction that accompanies rereading and talking about strategies that can help the team learn more words.

By now, students have reread the text several times—close reading, text features and structures, question formulation, class discussions, summarization, peer reading, and roundtable reviews—each time finding more information, integrating knowledge and ideas, and learning more words. This type of interaction and constant revisiting of the text for different purposes help ELs accelerate their vocabulary and facility with grammatical structures due to all of the subconscious repetition.

Steps 10–12: Writing in the Content Areas

Skill in writing is a predictor of academic success and a basic requirement for participation in civic life and global economy (Graham & Perin, 2007). English learners are not the only low-achieving writers, however. About 70 percent of students in any classroom are in need of explicit writing skills development (Graham & Perin, 2007). When we visit elementary classrooms and read students' writing samples on the bulletin boards, we see the limitations of conceptual information, grammatical structures, and the overwhelming use of the same words over and over. When we visit secondary schools, we rarely see students' writing anywhere. Nor do we see explicit instruction modeling how students are to execute the writing assignments individually, usually at home.

If middle and high school teachers have about one hundred students to see in a day, it is very unlikely that they will spend quality time reading those assignments and giving powerful feedback for improvement. ELs rarely get additional help with writing. Most assistance is for oral English development, maybe some phonics, and translations to help understand content. Fill-in-the-blank worksheets typically represent writing instruction for ELs. Hence, explicit writing instruction at the secondary level will benefit all students but especially ELs. Plus, it will save teachers a lot of headaches and tears when it comes to grading everyone's writing.

Research on writing is scarce. Nevertheless, Steve Graham and Dolores Perin (2007) recommend these key elements, which have positive effect sizes.

1. Writing Strategies, which involves teaching students strategies for planning, revising and editing their compositions.

2. Summarization, which involves explicitly and systematically teaching students how to summarize texts.

3. Collaborative Writing, which uses instructional arrangements in which adolescents work together to plan, draft, revise, and edit their compositions.

4. Specific Product Goals, which assigns students specific, reachable goals for the writing they are to complete.

5. Word Processing, which uses computers and word processors as instructional supports for writing assignments.

6. Sentence Combining, which involves teaching students to construct more complex, sophisticated sentences.

7. Prewriting, which engages students in activities designed to help them generate or organize ideas for their composition.

8. Inquiry Activities, which engages students in analyzing immediate, concrete data to help them develop ideas and content for a particular writing task.

9. Study of Models, which provides students opportunities to read, analyze, and emulate models of good writing.

10. Writing for Content Learning, which uses writing as a tool for learning content material. (pp. 4–5)

Additionally, the authors state that writing workshops, which are prevalent in most schools with ELs, have no positive effect sizes for any students (Graham & Perin, 2007). We recommend that Graham and Perin's evidence-based instructional strategies be combined in ways that show clear results for improving students' writing. The ExC-ELL Model (Calderón, 2007, 2009, 2011a, 2011b, 2012, 2013; Committee on the Study of Teacher Preparation Programs in the United States, 2010) tested the key elements and finds the following five-component framework to be the most effective for ELs and low-achieving writers. We've added references to the CCSS to recommend how the writing components can address these students' needs.

1. **Writing strategies for content-area learning:** This style of writing helps ELs anchor their language, literacy, and content learning. The Common Core anchor standards and high school standards for literacy in history and social studies, science, and technical subjects provide guidelines and specificity for teaching writing. For example, various standards call for students to cite specific textual evidence to support analysis of science and technical texts; determine central ideas or conclusions; and summarize complex concepts, processes, or information presented in a text by paraphrasing them in simpler but still accurate terms (NGA & CCSSO, 2010a). Thus, the instruction that a teacher has provided, as recommended in the vocabulary, reading, and after-reading chapters in this book, sets the stage for this type of writing.

2. **Modeling and inquiry activities:** Teachers use a mentor text or a concrete experience for ELs to read, discuss, analyze, and emulate after the teacher has pretaught key vocabulary, conducted a think-aloud to highlight aspects of the writing expected from students, and facilitated partner reading with summarization and other after-reading activities. For example, the CCSS call for students to follow precisely a complex multistep procedure when carrying out experiments, taking measurements, or performing technical tasks and analyze the specific results based on explanations in the text (NGA & CCSSO, 2010a).

3. **Additional vocabulary instruction:** The CCSS call for teachers to introduce accurate and knowledgeable claims, distinguish the claims from alternate or opposing claims, and create an organization that logically sequences the claims (NGA & CCSSO, 2010a). Thus, teachers must provide words, phrases, and clauses as well as varied syntax to link the major section of the text, create cohesion, and clarify the relationships between claims and reasons, between reasons and evidence, and between claims and counterclaims.

4. **Collaborative writing and writing strategies:** The use of such strategies, when ELs are placed in a heterogeneous team of three or four, helps students learn to draft, revise, and edit with assistance from peers. These skills then transfer to independent use.

5. **Specific product goals:** Teachers must clarify the goals for student products. For instance, they can create a rubric that states the language and writing standards and that differentiates for language proficiency levels.

After partner reading, students will be curious about additional words they found. This is also an opportunity to highlight features that are found in the text. For instance, if superlatives are found (such as *the largest* or *most perplexing*), this is an opportunity to give more examples of when to use the *-est* suffix or the word *most*. They can also find synonyms that provide more specificity for simple words, grammatical structures, and other features of language that you want to see in their writing.

Summary

All middle and high school mathematics, science, social studies, and electives teachers can be academic language and reading comprehension teachers. They can also teach text-based writing using their classroom mentor texts. Once they integrate the instructional sequence described in the previous chapters, they begin to see the benefits this affords all students, not just ELs. Whole schools will see the changes in student academic gains. Administrators will find classroom observations to be more gratifying when they see 100 percent of the students engaged in authentic learning. Students' attendance and punctuality will be evidence that they actually like learning this way.

CHAPTER 5

MATHEMATICS INSTRUCTION FOR ENGLISH LEARNERS

By Maria Trejo

Mathematics teachers struggle to develop lessons that incorporate all three instructional components that ELs need: (1) grade-level academic English, (2) mastery of English literacy, and (3) mathematics content. There is often a lack of appropriate instructional materials, timely professional development, and time to learn new strategies. It is difficult for teachers to find free time to meet and articulate instructional goals, discuss commonalities among the high school curriculum, and assess individual students' needs. Secondary ELs are particularly at risk, as they may have less time to learn academic English, to learn all content from the standards, and to meet graduation requirements.

Yet, according to Talia Milgrom-Elcott (2013), "STEM learning will enable our children to grow our economy, discover new cures, solve old mysteries, and address the most pressing challenges of tomorrow" (p. 2). Why should our ELs not be able to address these challenges as well? The STEM Education Coalition's (2012) *Statement of Core Policy Principles* includes a strong emphasis on hands-on, inquiry-based learning activities that could be very successful for ELs, such as learning about the engineering design process, working directly with STEM professionals through internships, and participating in field experiences and STEM-related competitions.

To more deeply explore the connection between literacy and STEM fields in relation to ELs, this chapter describes strategies to increase ELs' mathematics achievement levels.

Mathematics and Literacy Skills for ELs

Jeremy Kilpatrick, Jane Swafford, and Bradford Findell (2001) write:

> For people to participate fully in society, they must know basic mathematics. Citizens who cannot reason mathematically are cut off from whole realms of human endeavor. Innumeracy deprives them not only of opportunity but also of competence in everyday tasks. (p. 1)

Knowledge of mathematics, science, and reading is critical for participating effectively in a global economy. According to the Organisation for Economic Co-operation and Development (OECD, 2012), among its thirty-four member countries, the United States ranked below average in mathematics (27th), science (20th), and reading (17th). The report also revealed that there has been no significant change in these performances over time (OECD, 2012). Too many students require remedial mathematics courses upon enrolling in colleges and universities. Kelsey Sheehy (2012), commenting on the results of college entrance exams, states that of the nearly 1.7 million high school graduates who took the ACT college entrance exam in 2012, only 23 percent of African American, Hispanic, and American Indian students met the mathematics benchmark.

The U.S. performance levels of ELs, in particular, are far below those of their English-proficient peers in mathematics, reading, and science. In states such as North Dakota, Wyoming, and Nebraska (U.S. Department of Education, 2013b), with large numbers of ELs and limited staff experience working with them, meeting ELs' academic needs is even more challenging. According to reports issued by the U.S. Department of Education (2013a), the world competitiveness of the United States is threatened as relatively few U.S. students pursue expertise in the STEM fields, there is an increasingly inadequate pipeline of teachers skilled in those subjects, and only 16 percent of U.S. high school seniors who are proficient in mathematics are also interested in a STEM career. The U.S. Department of Education (2013a) further reports that even among those who do go on to pursue a college major in the STEM fields, only about half choose to work in a related career.

The importance of learning the language of mathematics has been taken for granted. A common observation is that addition is addition in any language, so there is no need to worry about teaching the language of mathematics to ELs because it transfers, and students will easily acquire it. Not true. Directions for mathematics problems, processes, symbols, and word problems are embedded in a language that most ELs do not understand.

Lowered expectations and watered-down courses have left ELs unable to catch up to their peers and unprepared for college or training programs. Experts point out that, based on data from the Second International Mathematics Study (SIMS) and the Third International Mathematics and Science Study (TIMSS), a traditional low-track, remedial curriculum actually depresses the mathematics performance of U.S. students rather than improving it (Cogan, Schmidt, & Wiley, 2001). Other studies find that when schools fail to provide all students with a rich, high-quality mathematics curriculum and qualified teachers, it results in large proportions of students failing mathematics and abandoning its study early in their high school careers (Mathematical Sciences Education Board, the Board on Mathematical Sciences, & National Research Council, 1989). Other experts show that providing low-achieving students with less-challenging courses does not result in academic success (Kifer, 1993). National councils and commissions agree that all students should master a more-challenging mathematics curriculum (Mathematical Sciences Education Board et al., 1989; National Council of Teachers of Mathematics [NCTM], 2012; Riley, 1997). But unfortunately, many students lack access to rich curriculum, quality teaching, and resources to help them reach high learning standards (Darling-Hammond, 2003). Most ELs are disproportionately impacted by low teacher expectations, lack of access due to language difficulties, and lack of enriched experiences dues to poverty.

Mathematics Standards for ELs

National standards, such as the Common Core State Standards (NGA & CCSSO, 2010c) and the Principles and Standards for School Mathematics (NCTM, 2012), may address the process of language acquisition and make connections to English language arts standards, but they do not provide enough instructional guidance to support literacy in other content areas.

Standards require students to not only learn functions and formulas but also demonstrate—both orally and in writing—a deeper understanding of key concepts, a variety of strategies to solve problems, and their thinking about the applications of mathematics and its relationship to other subject areas, such as engineering, science, and technology. Applications and conversations are encouraged. The standards place more emphasis on critical thinking than memorization and require more opportunities for collaborative learning. Thus, ELs and struggling readers will need a deeper command of oral language and vocabulary to understand complex ideas, ask higher-level questions, discuss multiple ways of solving problems, and generally express what they know. If students are not learning academic language, their reading ability, independent reading skills, and mental processes will be affected and delayed (Marulis

& Neuman, 2010). The CCSS also reiterate the importance of students acquiring a rich and varied vocabulary to succeed in all content areas (NGA & CCSSO, 2010a). Consider the following mathematics word problem example (figure 5.1) and what an EL reports as problematic.

Luis is struggling to show how much mathematics he knows, how much he does not understand, and how to express his frustrations. It seems that when he does the problems in algebra and geometry, he learns the formulas and steps fairly quickly, but when he needs to solve word problems, he has no idea how to begin. Here are two examples that he has communicated to his teachers.

Example A

Problem: Find the area of a rectangle that is 3 inches high with a 4-inch base.

Luis's response: No problem. I can solve this.

Solution: $A = bh$. $A = 4 \times 3 = 12$.

Example B

Problem: A pathway 50 feet long and 5 feet wide is paved with bricks measuring 8 inches by 4 inches. The bricks are on sale and cost $9.50 a dozen. How many bricks are needed for the pathway?

Luis's response: BIG problem. I have no clue where to begin.

Figure 5.1: Sample EL difficulties.

Teachers must address language and skills of ELs like Luis while also identifying and preteaching new vocabulary or phrases, addressing the language and symbols of mathematics, and discussing information that students need and don't need.

Those involved in the development of the CCSS agree that all students need to acquire a set of core skills; the authors envision the following six goals for all students across content areas (NGA & CCSSO, 2010a).

1. Standards that define what students should understand and be able to do

2. Students being able to show their understanding of the material by justifying their answers or positions

3. A curriculum that focuses on fewer skills and addresses them in greater depth

4. Standards that express coherence by building on students' understanding and prior knowledge and introducing new topics from grade to grade

5. Students being able to learn procedures fluently, develop a deep conceptual understanding, and solve problems

6.   More time devoted to deep thinking and understanding of concepts, with time to reread, redraft, discuss, analyze, and solve problems

Research supports that effective instruction in general is the foundation for effective instruction for ELs as well (Slavin et al., 2011). However, while good instruction for all may be the base, it is not sufficient to ensure that ELs learn both the content material to keep up with their native English-speaking counterparts and gain grade-level academic English in a timely manner (Calderón, 2012). ELs need additional support. Experts find that ELs need added time and specific strategies to meet each standard, prepare for college or training programs, and develop higher-level content and analytical skills (Slavin et al, 2011).

For example, the overarching Common Core's Standards for Mathematical Practice address eight areas that students should develop to foster mathematical understanding, expertise, skills, and knowledge—essentially what all students, but especially ELs, need to know and do (NGA & CCSSO, 2010c). Following are these eight standards with tips for enhancing them for ELs, using Example B in figure 5.1.

1.   **Make sense of problems and persevere in solving them:** The teacher identifies and teaches key vocabulary words or phrases. Students practice new vocabulary and start oral discussions with peers to anticipate what the problem is actually asking. *I need to find out how many bricks are needed. What key facts are provided?*

2.   **Reason abstractly and quantitatively:** The teacher models think-alouds and partner reading. Students practice and discuss with partners. *Is my answer going to be expressed in numbers, percentages, money, feet, or inches? Do I need to convert inches to feet or feet to inches? Why is the cost of bricks included?*

3.   **Construct viable arguments and critique the reasoning of others:** Students think and discuss with a group or partner. *The answer has to be in numbers because it asks how many bricks. So, the cost of bricks has nothing to do with the problem.*

4.   **Model with mathematics:** The teacher directs students to illustrate how they would solve the problem using square pegs, drawings, formulas, or models. *I need to know the formula for area. I will need to do some multiplication or division. I can draw equal-size squares to sketch the pathway.*

5.   **Use appropriate tools strategically:** The teacher makes sure students have all the tools needed to solve the problem and that they understand how to use each tool. *I can sketch it using a ruler to visualize the space and then do the calculations with my calculator. I can use computer animations that may help me get the answer.*

6. **Attend to precision:** The teacher helps students determine what information is necessary and what isn't. She has them look at the answer choices and try to delete wrong answers. Students also determine again if they need to make various calculations and conversions. *I need to reread to ensure that I understand the problem correctly and have considered all key information. Why do they tell me the size of bricks? Why do they give me information in both inches and feet?*

7. **Look for and make use of structure:** Students check their work and ensure they followed each step of the process. *I better remember to reread and see if my answers look logical. My answer has to be the number of bricks, not a figure expressed in inches or feet.*

8. **Look for and express regularity in repeated reasoning:** The teacher reminds students to discuss with peers the steps, solutions, and a proposed answer. *Is there extra information? Did I understand all instructions and vocabulary? Did I eliminate wrong answers and unneeded information? Did I make the calculations and conversions required to solve the problem? Did I read, reread, outline the problem, and then solve the problem?*

Essentially, instruction must be explicit and well planned. NCTM's (2012) standard 5, "Impact on Student Learning," is an example of an instructional expectation for teachers:

> Effective teachers of secondary mathematics provide evidence demonstrating that as a result of their instruction, secondary students' conceptual understanding, procedural fluency, strategic competence, adaptive reasoning, and application of major mathematics concepts in varied contexts have increased. . . . They show that new student mathematical knowledge has been created as a consequence of their ability to engage students in mathematical experiences that are developmentally appropriate, require active engagement, and include mathematics-specific technology in building new knowledge. (p. 4)

The skills described in standard 5 require that students—including ELs—have a rich, high-level working academic vocabulary and deep knowledge of the content area to successfully engage in manipulating mathematical concepts and be strategic at solving problems.

Literacy Strategies for Word Problems

Many word problems have extensive verbiage and require multiple mathematical applications, critical thinking, explanations, and steps to finding correct answers.

This complexity is very challenging for ELs and struggling readers. Teachers need to ensure students understand key vocabulary and core statements, don't get lost in the storyline, identify needed and extra information, and determine what the text is asking in order to select the appropriate mathematical procedures and answers.

Teachers often share that students in general are not interested in mathematics. Many students struggle with it, hate it, or avoid it. They do not see the need for mathematics or its application to their daily lives. Relevant examples of how mathematics impact students' daily decisions and purchases can be strong motivators. For instance, a majority of teens (53 percent) report that they want to learn more about managing their money (Capital One Financial Corporation, 2010). Discussions about personal finances help students develop several of the Common Core's Standards for Mathematical Practice, particularly "Make sense of problems and persevere in solving them," "Reason abstractly and quantitatively," and "Construct viable arguments and critique the reasoning of others."

Real-world problems, such as finances, are extremely helpful for ELs and struggling readers, because they help build vocabulary, confidence, and mathematical thinking and processes. Students will be highly engaged, as long as the problems are real and relevant. Also, such strategies align with the fourth Standard for Mathematical Practice: "Model with mathematics. Mathematically proficient students can apply mathematics to solve problems in everyday life, society, and the workplace" (NGA & CCSSO, 2010c).

To help ELs both complete relevant problems and develop academic discourse, teachers should have students work in pairs. They then select one problem and read it to the whole class. Next, they should ask students to discuss key words or phrases important to solving the problem, possible steps to solving the problem, and possible answers to the problem. This is all done orally to help ELs.

Discuss Key Words and Phrases

There are several ways to help ELs recognize key words and phrases. The instruction can be:

- Part of daily structured and focused mathematical conversations that students conduct in pairs or triads

- Part of preteaching, in which teachers select specific words before reading

- Part of the process of solving problems—students ask each other or they ask the teacher to explain new words

- Focused on the language in the instructions, tests, quizzes, graphs, or charts in textbooks
- Taught while reviewing sample tests

A sample lesson plan in appendix D (page 115) provides additional strategies for incorporating vocabulary throughout the lessons.

Here's an example to enhance ELs' understanding.

> Pedro makes $25.00 an hour, and he gets a $2.50 raise. He would like to know what part to whole is the additional raise in fractions or percentage.

The teacher reviews and preteaches key vocabulary: *part to whole*, *additional*, and *raise*. Students then practice the new vocabulary and start oral discussions with peers to anticipate what the problem is actually asking. Finally, the teacher uses the seven-step vocabulary process described in chapter 2 (page 35) to reinforce this vocabulary.

Discuss Possible Steps to Solve the Problem

It is crucial to determine if students are having difficulties with the functions of mathematics or the symbols and the language of mathematics. It may be all of these for ELs and struggling readers. Providing daily opportunities to discuss and process word problems greatly enhances students' progress.

EL students must develop semantic awareness in daily mathematical conversations. Consider a word problem that addresses a current event, such as the rise in college tuition. After preteaching such terms as *fees, tuition, allowance, units of study, living allowance*, and *rental leases*, the teacher asks her students to discuss the issue, why it is a problem, how they would solve it, and how it is relevant to their personal lives and their communities. She gives students three to five minutes to talk over the problem and come up with a variety of solutions. This activity is all oral, and students conduct their discussions in pairs or small groups.

Another powerful strategy is to teach students to practice reading word problems, instructions, graphs, and charts using read-aloud and partner reading. They need not solve the problem but read with accuracy, discuss what each sentence is saying, determine what it's asking, and identify the best strategy or steps for solving the problem.

Discuss Possible Answers to the Problem

At this point, the students are ready to pursue an answer. They need to determine what mathematical procedures are required to solve the problem. For example, will they need to do some subtraction to compare existing tuition fees with proposed fee increases? Will they also need to do multiplication, such as new fees per unit multiplied by the number of average units that students normally would take to determine the new costs? In addition, they will need to determine how the correct answer should be expressed. Will it be in dollars, units, or percentages?

Discuss Sample Problems

Some teachers find that presenting a daily problem to talk through works well. Following are several problems to get teachers started.

The examples in figure 5.2 help teachers prepare students for state exams that are aligned with state and local standards. Teachers present a variety of word problems so that students can practice formats, multiple-choice exams, and guesstimation of answers. As students read, discuss, and try to solve the sample problems, teachers observe the students to assess difficulties that they might have during the tests; for example, is the problem key vocabulary, math procedures, rushing to solve problems without carefully reading and planning out how to set up the problem, or other individual issues? Based on the observations, the teachers can review, reteach, or practice additional test-taking strategies. The teacher may select to work with the whole class or with individual students, depending the students' needs.

Number Sense (Grade 7)
Peter was interested in buying a basketball. By the time he saved enough money, everything in the sporting-goods store had been marked up by 15%. Two weeks later, however, the same store had a sale, and everything was sold at a 15% discount. Peter immediately bought the ball, figuring that he was paying even less than before the prices were raised. Was he mistaken?
Measurement and Geometry (Grade 7)
A bucket is put under two faucets. If one faucet is turned on alone, the bucket will be filled in 3 minutes; if the other is turned on, the bucket will be filled in 2 minutes. If both are turned on, how many seconds will it take to fill the bucket?
Algebra 1 (Grades 8–12)
I started with a number and applied a four-step process: (1) add 13, (2) multiply by 2, (3) take the square root, and (4) take the reciprocal. The result is 1. • What number did I start with? • If I start with the number $4x$, write a formula that gives the result of the four-step process.

Source: California Department of Education, 2013c.

Figure 5.2: Sample state exam problems.

See figure 5.3 (page 86) for examples of personal finance word problems from the annual competitions of the National Financial Capability Challenge sponsored by the U.S. Department of the Treasury and the U.S. Department of Education (Yaron, 2011). These competitions motivate students to learn about money and how to take control of their financial futures.

1. John wants to buy a car. One car that he looks at costs $20,000, and the other costs $18,000. If sales tax is 8 percent, and he is financing the entire purchase at 10 percent simple interest for one year, what is the actual difference in cost of these two cars?

   A. $2,000

   B. $2,160

   C. $2,360

   D. $2,376

2. Steven's monthly net pay is $1,200. He wants to save 10 percent of his income each month. If his monthly expenses (except for entertainment) are $800, how much can he spend each month on entertainment?

   A. $580

   B. $382

   C. $280

   D. $220

3. How much would Bill save each year if he switched from a $4 cup of coffee each morning to a cup of tea (50 cents for a teabag and hot water)?

   A. $182.50

   B. $912.50

   C. $1,277.50

   D. $1,460

Source: Yaron, 2011.

Figure 5.3: Sample financial problems.

Teachers can find such examples online or create their own. A variation to providing students with a daily problem would be to ask them to draft their own word problems and submit them for use in class. Using *Bloom's Taxonomy Interpreted for Mathematics* (Shorser, 2013), teachers can have students develop word problems at various levels of rigor. The taxonomy helps students become familiar with questions or prompts that hint at the complexity of the word problems and that reflect those of tests and exams. For example, most students might select or develop simple *who, what, how much* word problems that require simple mathematical procedures. But most tests include problems that require multiple decisions and procedures to find the correct answer. Many word problems include superfluous information to confuse students. The teacher can create a problem bank to use for daily lessons.

Summary

Students' abilities to solve problems depend on their understanding of specific words and symbols that may have different meaning or multiple meanings in mathematics. Mathematics literacy, in particular, needs explicit instruction. ELs need added time to learn mathematics language, symbols, concepts, and processes.

Mathematics illiteracy is just as sad as challenges with reading. Students need mathematics to negotiate cost-effective prices for all purchases, from a candy bar to a home or car. Knowing mathematics is indispensable to almost all careers and professions, and those who pursue higher education must be able to select colleges and universities where they can attain the highest level of academic and work preparation—at the lowest cost.

Schools need to continue to improve curriculum and instructional practices and provide the resources necessary to ensure that all students acquire a strong foundation in mathematical thinking and its applications.

Next, we'll look at the role of literacy in another STEM field: science.

CHAPTER 6

SCIENCE INSTRUCTION FOR ENGLISH LEARNERS

By Maria Trejo

ow performance in science mirrors the low performance in English language arts and mathematics for ELs. The Next Generation Science Standards (NGSS; NGSS Lead States, 2013) require a more sophisticated level of academic language, and if ELs have poor or limited literacy and academic skills in English, they cannot participate in scholarly and engaging lessons.

ELs need multiple opportunities to solve problems, generate hypotheses, make effective connections between ideas, incorporate visuals and graphics, construct and answer high-level questions, and gain a sense of accomplishment (Chamot & O'Malley, 1994). Teachers must provide them more time and opportunities to read and comprehend informational texts and write grammatically correct expository essays. Instruction for ELs should focus on academic vocabulary development, small-group instruction, cooperative learning strategies, and additional time to practice new skills and new language. Where possible, science instruction should also incorporate ELA, ELD, and mathematics standards.

The NGSS offer a new opportunity for English learners to acquire yet another area of rich, academic vocabulary; expand analytical skills; and learn about the field of science. They include three dimensions for each standard (NGSS Lead States, 2013).

1. **Performance:** The behaviors of scientists and practices that engineers engage in to build models, theories, or systems

2. **Foundations:** Concepts that have applications across science dimensions and other content areas

3. **Coherence:** Fields that focus the science curriculum and assessment for each grade level

For instance, both the crosscutting concepts and the science and engineering practices within the NGSS offer numerous opportunities for language development. The seven crosscutting concepts help students understand and connect core ideas across disciplines and grade bands (NGSS Lead States, 2013).

1. Patterns

2. Cause and effect

3. Scale, proportion, and quantity

4. Systems and system models

5. Energy and matter

6. Structure and function

7. Stability and change

The eight science and engineering practices mirror those of professional scientists and engineers (NGSS Lead States, 2013).

1. Asking questions and defining problems

2. Developing and using models

3. Planning and carrying out investigations

4. Analyzing and interpreting data

5. Using mathematics and computational thinking

6. Constructing explanations and designing solutions

7. Engaging in argument from evidence

8. Obtaining, evaluating, and communicating information

The NGSS also strongly encourage applying key skills found in mathematics and English language arts to science and engineering. These include:

- Constructing explanations and engaging in arguments from evidence

- Understanding how to use crosscutting concepts (patterns, structure, and function) in science disciplines, such as structure, properties of matter, earth materials, and systems

Once students learn to recognize and apply the concept of patterns in mathematics, they should also be able to see patterns in science, art, technology, and mechanical drawing. In English language arts, they learn about the structure of cause and effect. When they master this structure, students should be able to use this critical-thinking skill in science, history, physical education, and other areas.

Thus, the NGSS are cognitively demanding but provide clear guidelines and support for the implementation of science instruction. They illustrate how science education can take place in classrooms, schools, the home, and the community, making science literacy a real-world experience.

Science Literacy in Real-World Situations

Given equitable learning opportunities, students from diverse backgrounds can use scientific practices and construct meaning in both science classrooms and informal settings (Lee, Quinn, & Valdés, 2013). Expected outcomes are similar to those in the Common Core ELA and mathematics standards: students must engage in argumentation from evidence; construct explanations; obtain, synthesize, evaluate, and communicate information; and build a knowledge base through content-rich texts across the three subject areas.

Project-based learning is a key strategy for students who lack background knowledge or academic vocabulary. The crosscutting concepts and science and engineering practices encourage the implementation of project-based instruction and challenge teachers to think beyond the classroom and its resources or money limitations and to start looking at resources and learning opportunities in local communities. Schools located near rivers, lakes, oceans, mountains, or forests have great venues to learn about wildlife, water conservation, and global warming. Schools near museums, aquariums, or zoos can expose students to careers and skills required to work in those areas. Schools located near cheese factories, canneries, farmer markets, car manufacturers, or culinary institutes can visit these places for students to learn how science, mathematics, technology, engineering, reading, and writing skills are interrelated and essential to develop those products.

Teachers must reach beyond classrooms, laboratories, videos, and books. ELs learn crosscutting concepts and skills when they can see their immediate application, since concrete experiences help ELs retain vocabulary and concepts at much higher rates than mere memorization.

Here, we present effective strategies to help increase ELs' comprehension, proficiency, and confidence so they succeed on both formal and informal assessments and in daily classroom activities.

Literacy Strategies for Science and Technical Subjects

Teachers will need to provide students with additional time to read and reread closely, practice newly learned strategies, discuss ideas, internalize key concepts, write and edit concept papers, and do challenging lessons. Effective instruction for ELs needs to include daily teaching of subject-specific terminology (tier three) but also other academic vocabulary (tiers one and two) to build literacy and understanding of concepts in each technical subject (Calderón, 2007).

Students need extra time to learn grade-level academic language, English literacy skills, key vocabulary, and concepts specific to science; extra assistance from teachers and other students in smaller cooperative learning groups; and hands-on, inquiry-based instruction that uses manipulatives or concrete props and is grounded in real-life situations. To meet these needs, teachers must consider a variety of strategies to ensure that ELs have equitable access to the NGSS, including:

- Citing specific textual evidence
- Making STEM concepts and professions concrete
- Asking strong questions
- Determining meaning of symbols, key terms, and phrases from a specific scientific or technical text
- Analyzing the author's purpose and structure
- Exploring visual quantitative or technical information
- Distinguishing among facts based on research findings
- Comparing and contrasting information

We'll discuss each of these strategies in depth here.

Citing Specific Textual Evidence

Teachers should ensure students understand how to record primary sources and report findings. They should also ask students to study important community issues and relevant themes using outside sources. For example, if students read something like "In the last few years, there have been many more sharks spotted closer to beaches where people swim. There have been more shark attacks in the summer," they can research using newspaper articles, textbooks, or online sources to identify probable causes for the increase in shark attacks. They can then investigate primary-source material by speaking with local experts, such as newspaper reporters, scientists, oceanographers, aquarium staff, and biologists. Students jot down their notes in journals, do quick writes, or write full reports summarizing the findings. With this activity, students practice the NGSS crosscutting concept of cause and effect and the science and engineering practices of asking questions and defining problems, planning and carrying out investigations, and analyzing and interpreting data (NGSS Lead States, 2013).

Making STEM Concepts and Professions Concrete

Often ELs have little or no background experience in what is being studied in the various content areas, nor do adults in their homes. The adults may have limited education, no college degrees, or limited exposure to a variety of professions. To help students concretize ideas and concepts, teachers can invite special speakers to share with students how scientific skills being learned in school connect to professions in STEM fields and college or how to be better consumers and family members. Students prepare by becoming familiar with the speakers' backgrounds. Teachers can help this process by introducing students to major vocabulary and concepts, having students read about the profession in general, and providing them with sentence and question starters related to the topic so that they maximize their understanding and participation. Speakers can help students focus their studies and preparation for various professions. Experts bring new points of view to the classroom. In addition to discussing their profession, they also often speak of their journey—of hard work, perseverance, and disappointments. These are all key values for students to learn. After speakers visit, students write summaries about what they have learned.

Asking Strong Questions

Research on the power of questioning and its impact on student reading often reveals that most students do not ask many questions while in learning settings, and most student- and teacher-posed questions tend to be shallow, including those from textbooks (Graesser, Ozuru, & Sullins, 2009). In addition, ELs and struggling readers tend to not ask many questions because they do not have the language or frames to do so. Teaching students to develop higher-order questioning during science instruction is a powerful instructional tool that helps develop a variety of skills, including making accurate summaries. Students have an opportunity to use the crosscutting concepts of patterns, structures, and functions. Learning to pose concise and clear questions helps students achieve the science and engineering practices of planning and carrying out investigations, analyzing and interpreting data, constructing explanations and designing conclusions, and obtaining, evaluating, and communicating information.

Open-ended questions stretch students' thinking and curiosity and help them focus their researching, learning, and fact finding and, ultimately, help them create accurate conclusions and summaries. To achieve this level of questioning, teachers need to provide examples of good questions—and then let students come up with their own questions—that activate prior knowledge, guide learning, and enhance comprehension. See figure 6.1 for sample questions.

Sample questions for prereading or preproject activities:

- What do I know about the topic I am going to study?
- How can this topic be of importance to me?
- What other subject am I studying that relates to this topic?
- What are two key facts that I would like to know when I finish this project?

(Students develop two more questions, paraphrase some of the preceding questions, or develop subcategories of the questions.)

Sample questions during reading and during the project process:

- What key points am I reading about?
- Am I stretching my knowledge or verifying what I knew before?
- How is this topic related to other topics that I am learning about?
- Do I agree with the author's point of view?
- Has technology affected this area?

(Students develop two more preliminary summaries, paraphrase some of the preceding questions, or develop subcategories of the questions.)

Sample questions to guide summaries or conclusions after reading or at the end of a project:

- Were my notions about this topic accurate? Explain.
- What were the most important skills and information I learned from this project?
- What can I conclude from what I have read or researched?

(Students develop summaries, outlines, and a list of facts to use during tests, share during oral conversations with various partners, or use as models for other research and assignments.)

Figure 6.1: Sample questions for prereading or preproject activities.

Determining Meaning of Symbols, Key Terms, and Phrases From a Specific Scientific or Technical Text

Planning extra time and many opportunities to practice new language will actually expedite the academic achievement for all students and specifically ELs (Calderón, 2007). The study of science requires a new vocabulary and a new application of familiar words in novel contexts. ELs may know some science terminology but may not be aware that words have different definitions in common use compared with scientific use, such as in *inquiry*, *solution*, and *assumption*. Teachers must take time to teach processing words in specific subjects, such as when comparing or summarizing after an experiment: *as opposed to, in many ways, another way, in contrast to, given that, as a result of,* and *in the same way.* They must also teach variations by explaining to students, for example, that in science, *another way* could be stated as *method, means, technique, approach, tactic,* or *representation.* Teachers must also devote time to teaching mathematical symbols, acronyms, and concepts such as *feet (ft.), centimeters (cm),* geometric graphics, formulas, equations, graphs, and scientific tables, while pointing out the different applications in each subject area.

Using science texts to enhance literacy skills can be most effective. Students learn more academic vocabulary in context and master different sentence patterns. They learn how authors develop and use models, plan and carry out investigations, and analyze and interpret data. For example, teachers can present the science and engineering practices of asking questions and defining problems and planning and carrying out investigations by modeling a think-aloud. The teacher can also model making connections to prior knowledge and connecting ideas across other subjects. To expedite comprehension, teachers can present pattern structures that students practice during the think-aloud and read-aloud activities.

Analyzing the Author's Purpose and Structure

Consider the following statement:

> If people migrate involuntarily (because of war, political or religious oppression or persecution, or climate challenges), and the receiving community accepts them and finds sustainable places for them in the community, their experiences in the new place can be a wonderful, life-giving opportunity. (Peyton, 2013, p. 3)

The teacher first explains that the author is presenting a cause-and-effect hypothesis ("If _____, their experiences of _____"). But the teacher also explains that immigrants can have positive experiences when "the community accepts them and finds sustainable places for them in the community." From these brief explanations, ELs acquire several lessons. They learn about text structure and author purpose. This helps students guide their reading and assignments by asking questions, such as "In what ways does the author say that immigrants are received? What new questions do I have? What else do I need to study further?"

Exploring Visual Quantitative or Technical Information

Teachers need to take much more time to explain and expose students to graphics, keys, charts, symbols, timelines, and maps in the pages students read. Additionally, they need to remind all students, and ELs in particular, that these elements are just as important as the narrative in the text. Most students gloss over or completely ignore information presented outside of the narrative. Many can only read simple pie or bar graphs. Text features can be especially helpful to ELs because they provide both language and graphics to assist with comprehension. If students are not taught to recognize, read, and use these elements, they cannot incorporate them into assignments. One powerful strategy that helps students appreciate the importance of visuals is to ask them to read a chapter or text and then graphically summarize it and present it in class. This activity is much more complex than it appears. To do it well, students will need to read the text, identify key ideas and details, and determine what symbols, diagrams, or graphs to use to illustrate key points and summaries.

Distinguishing Among Facts Based on Research Findings

Scientific work requires students to present what they read and learn, not what they think. Facts must substantiate any personal opinions. Students need to know how to identify actual facts or findings from observations and published works and then how to refer to them when doing their research. Teachers can start teaching ELs this distinction by discussing the subtleties of key words such as *may, shall, will, could, was, appeared,* and *intended.* Next, the teacher explains that these words express degrees of truth and presents them in sentences to discuss: "Because the DNA tests were inconclusive, he thought that he may not have three brothers. He had jumped 4.5 and 5.2 feet during bad weather, so he believed that he could jump 5 feet in good weather, if he practiced. He hypothesized that because many of his peers, who were less studious than he, were going to college, he might be able to go also. He experimented taking different routes from his home to work to see if he could be on time, but he did not understand that he did not get going early enough until he started to time himself." To ensure clarity, the teacher highlights such phrases when students are reading: "Demographers estimate that there are *approximately* 2.5 million immigrants. He *may be* an immigrant because he is not a U.S. citizen. The law states that we *shall* acquire permits before drilling for oil." Finally, students underline qualifiers when they appear in text questions: "Do water levels <u>always</u> rise when it rains? What is the <u>best</u> answer to the question above? Do <u>all</u> pit bulls attack people?" Learning to recognize these cues will help students read and write more accurately.

Students also need to learn the difference between research, copying, and plagiarism. Teachers must clarify and model how to cite research and quote authors, as well as when to paraphrase with citation.

These activities will help ELs be more precise and learn how to distinguish among facts, approximations, and estimations when they write. They also help ELs make educated guesses when they take tests.

Comparing and Contrasting Information

Students need familiarity with comparing and contrasting information to successfully understand scientific texts. Words texts use for comparing and contrasting may be *difference, similarities, commonalities, alike, similar, in contrast to, compared to*, and so on. Teachers can use documents or research articles that include these words to teach students. For example, "The differences among rivers, lakes, and reservoirs are _____," "Molecules, in contrast to cells are _____," "Oceans and islands are similar in that they both _____." During practice, the topic of the text may not be as important as a student's ability to identify the processing words and the text structures the author uses. To help students make sense of the various sources of information—within and outside of a text—teachers should familiarize students with graphic organizers. Graphic organizers help students visually relate ideas by using single words, short statements, or even complex sentences or paragraphs to compare and contrast findings.

By using these strategies, teachers will ensure that ELs have the same access to the NGSS as their peers without diluting content. Teachers should explore each of these strategies to see which will work best in their classrooms with their students. See appendix E (page 123) for a sample science lesson.

Summary

Science, technology, engineering, and mathematics are often taught in isolation from one another and from other high school courses. Because students often do not have strong skills or background in each individual area, teachers must decide between covering material in depth or providing multiple opportunities and adequate time for English learners and struggling readers to access the material. However, skills necessary for STEM fields are not unique to each area in real practice. They are applied in interrelated ways in most jobs and professions. When students learn how the NGSS crosscutting concepts and science and engineering practices are applied, learning becomes much more interesting and relevant.

ELs with limited educational backgrounds and poor academic language need hands-on activities. Textbook-based instruction is the most difficult and least effective because it is abstract and foreign. Instead, we encourage teachers to use the strategies in this chapter to plan interactive project-based learning experiences for students, to rely on community resources, and to take advantage of cooperative learning and small-group strategies to ensure that all students are participating and learning.

NEXT STEPS

Education reformers have been searching for decades to find the silver bullet that fixes the system and creates a learner-centered, differentiated, integrated, interactive, and inclusive learning environment that better prepares the diverse student population to be college and career ready.

We should know by now that there is no silver bullet. Yet, as we have discussed in these pages, there are still ways to achieve our dream of education reform. We just need to be smart about how to select the best approach for *all* of our students. As you reflect on the various chapters of this book, consider the following five questions.

1. What CCSS, SEL competencies (self-awareness, self-management, social awareness, relationship skills, and responsible decision making), and 21st century skills (critical thinking, communication, collaboration, and creativity) can you integrate with your regular teaching strategies?

2. Does this approach align with the academic standards and incorporate SEL and 21st century skills?

3. Are there other teachers in your school who have integrated EL instructional strategies and resources into their teaching practices? Are you exchanging information on teaching, learning, and materials that could enhance your teaching effectiveness?

4. What approaches can you use to create a safe and caring classroom environment that promotes EL participation?

5. How has your school utilized instructional technology to support ELs' English language acquisition? Which software has been the most effective in accelerating language learning?

The key to successfully implementing a caring and inclusive learning environment where students feel welcomed, valued, and safe to contribute to the overall classroom climate lies in the degree to which teachers are able to model the very skills that we want students to learn. For instance, collaboration and cooperation allow teachers more opportunities to exchange ideas and address the most challenging classroom and school instructional issues. Teachers modeling the five core SEL competencies takes practice, persistence, and a realignment of thinking on who is or isn't "college material." Being able to come to terms with one's own thinking in judging student potential is the first essential step in gaining greater self-awareness, which will increase understanding of the other SEL core competencies. Changing how we see all ELs' potential is a major step in creating a more inclusive culture that will ultimately empower ELs to want to learn and to be successful.

APPENDIX A

TEXT FEATURES AND STRUCTURES

The reproducibles in this section help ELs complete peer summaries and writing assignments and participate in class discussions. Students can carry these in their folders or tape them to their desks or tables when they work in teams. Some teachers also like to laminate them and put them in bins where all students can access them during discussions and writing activities.

Clarifying Text Structure With Tier Two Words and Phrases

Text Structure	Tier Two Words and Phrases (Also known as signal or transition words)
Description • Denotes a specific topic and its attributes • Rich and descriptive details support main ideas	above, across, all, also, appears to be, as an example, behind, below, beside, by observing, characteristics are, for example, for instance, in addition, in back of, in front of, it means, most, most important, near, on top of, looks like, over, some, such as, to the left or right
Sequence and Process • Provides information and events in a specific order • Order of details convey specific meaning or explanation	additionally, after, after that, afterward, another, at _____ (time), before, during, finally, first, following, initially, last, later, subsequently, over the course of, meanwhile, next , not long after, once, on _____ (date), preceding, then, today, when, immediately, until, in
Problem-Solution • Identifies problems and provides solutions • Describes the problem and solution with supporting details	accordingly, answer, as a result, because, challenge, decide, fortunately, if . . . then, issue, one reason is, outcome is, problem, so, so that, solution, the problem is solved by, therefore, thus, trouble, unfortunately, despite, dilemma is, resolved by
Cause and Effect • Tells an event or action and the reasons it happened • Explains cause—why something happened • Explains effect—what happened	as a result, because of, accordingly, if, if . . . then, consequently, due to, effects of, for this, for this reason, in order to, is caused by, lead to, leads to, since, so, so that, thereby, therefore, thus, when . . . then, responsible for, may be due to
Compare and Contrast • Gives the similarities and differences of two or more items, ideas, objects, or places • Examines how things are alike or different by drawing on specific details	also, although, as opposed to, as well as, both, but, compared to, compared with, by contrast, different, different from, either . . . or, however, in comparison, on the other hand, in contrast, instead of, like, likewise, resembles, same, same as, similar, similarly, too, unlike, while, whereas, yet

Source: Adapted from Fisher, D., Frey, N., & Lapp, D. (2008). Shared readings: Modeling comprehension, vocabulary, text structures, and text features for older readers. The Reading Teacher, 61(7), 548–557, p. 89.

Organizing Information With Supporting Facts

Questions Answered	Common Formats	Main Idea or Thesis Example	Tier Two Words (Shares signal words with cause and effect)
• What is the viewpoint? • What evidence supports or disclaims the viewpoint?	Essays, speeches, newspaper editorials, and nonfiction articles (These may be in the form of an argument.)	• There are consequences for breaking federal rules regarding items permitted on board passenger airplanes. • Middle schools that require students to wear uniforms outperform other middle schools with the same demographics.	always, in fact, as a matter of fact, because of, clearly, generally, additionally, however, for instance, for example, it could be argued, most convincing, never, conclusively, not only . . . but also, often, typically, furthermore, truly, theory, argument, in conclusion

Providing Information Via Lists, Examples, and Features

Questions Answered	Common Genres	Main Idea or Thesis Example	Tier Two Words (Often same as sequence words but ideas are not dependent on chronological order)
• What examples support the main idea? • What proof, backup, or support is provided?	History, art history, social sciences, and political science	School counselors experience a number of scheduling problems that must be solved before students are assigned to classes.	one example, another, additionally, after, afterward, during, finally, first, second, third, following, initially, last, later, meanwhile, next, preceding, then, when, subsequently, moreover, in fact, besides

Writing and Reading Arguments

Support claims for argumentation include:

- Common knowledge
- Expert opinion
- Experimental evidence
- Factual information
- Additional information to back the claim

Sample tier two vocabulary for arguments includes:

- Argument
- Arrange
- Backup information
- Conditions
- Decide
- Deduce
- Define
- Elaborate
- Establish
- Evidence
- In contrast
- Objective
- On the grounds
- On the one hand
- On the other hand
- Prove
- Relationship
- Specific quote
- They shape
- Under these circumstances

Errors to avoid when writing arguments include:

- Misinformation
- Faulty logic
- Weak reference
- Misunderstanding of concept
- Inaccurate information
- Topic changes
- Attacks
- Untrue or biased information
- Appeals to emotions
- Unpreparedness

APPENDIX B

SUMMARY RUBRIC

Students can use this rubric to assess or keep track of their summaries based on text structure. During partner summaries, while one student reads and summarizes, the other can check the list and look for other possible additions or corrections. Teachers can write each of these categories on separate cards, laminate them, or place them in a binder for easy use.

Idea and details:

- Did I include all the main ideas?
- Did I include important details that match each main idea?
- Could I leave anything else out and still tell the reader what is important?

Cause and effect:

- Did I include the main causes and effects?
- Did I include important details and explain them?
- Could I leave anything else out and still tell the reader what is important?

Story:

- Did I include the main characters?
- Did I include the main characters' problems?
- Did I include the ways the main characters tried to solve the problems?
- Did I include the climax?
- Did I include what happened after the climax resolution?
- Could I leave anything else out and still tell the reader all the basic parts of the story?

Descriptive:

- Did I include only the main things the text describes?
- Did I include important details that match the main points?
- Could I leave anything else out and still tell the reader what is important?

Problem and solution:

- Did I include the main problems and solutions?
- Did I include the important details and explain them?
- Could I leave anything else out and still tell the reader what is important?

Compare and contrast:

- Did I include the main areas that the text compared and contrasted?
- Did I include the important details and explain them?
- Could I leave anything else out and still tell the reader what is important?

Sequential:

- Did I arrange all the main points or ideas as in the original?
- Did I include the important details and explain them?
- Could I leave anything else out and still tell the reader what is important?

Source: Adapted from Czarnecki, J. G. (2001). Summary checklists for different text structures. Accessed at www.thinkport.org/73bec609-f1cd-427f-8602-c632b4d0bb74.asset on February 13, 2015.

SAMPLE SOCIAL STUDIES LESSON: HISTORICAL THINKING

Subject: History

Title of mentor text and ancillary materials: "Critical Thinking: A Lesson From the Past on What Matters" by John A. Marino, Professor Emeritus, University of California, San Diego*

Content Standards

North Carolina Essential Standards for American History II

AH2.H.1.2: Use Historical Comprehension to:

1. Reconstruct the literal meaning of a historical passage.

2. Differentiate between historical facts and historical interpretations.

3. Analyze data in historical maps.

4. Analyze visual, literary, and musical sources.

AH2.H.1.3: Use Historical Analysis and Interpretation to:

1. Identify issues and problems of the past.

2. Consider multiple perspectives of various peoples of the past.

3. Evaluate competing historical narratives and debates among historians.

---

* We would like to thank the late Professor Marino for sharing his view of historical thinking.

4. Evaluate the influence of the past on contemporary issues (Public Schools of North Carolina, 2010, p. 3)

Common Core State Standards for English Language Arts and Literacy in History / Social Studies, Science, and Technical Subjects

RH.9–10.2: Determine the central ideas or information of a primary or secondary source; provide an accurate summary of how key events or ideas develop over the course of the text.

RH.9–10.4: Determine the meaning of words and phrases as they are used in a text, including vocabulary describing political, social, or economic aspects of history/social science.

WHST.9–10.2: Write informative/explanatory texts, including the narration of historical events, scientific procedures/experiments, or technical processes. (NGA & CCSSO, 2010a)

English Language Development Standards

Standard 5: English language learners *communicate* information, ideas, and concepts necessary for academic success in the content area of *Social Studies*. (World-Class Instructional Design and Assessment Consortium [WIDA], 2012, p. 3)

Preteaching Vocabulary and Discourse

(Twelve minutes)

Preteach five to six targeted words or clusters per reading segment that are key to comprehension, discussions, and text-based writing. See table C.1.

Methods and Procedures

For the following team-building activities, form heterogeneous teams of four students, mixing English learners and native English speakers. There can be a team of five for a newcomer EL. Each team develops a team name using one of the vocabulary words or phrases and creates a sign with its team name and its members. Throughout the lesson, use a discourse strategy—such as four corners, clock buddies, circle of friends, or elbow partners—and general team discussions to ensure understanding.

Teacher Read-Aloud, Think-Aloud

(Three minutes)

Before beginning a read-aloud and think-aloud, explain the standard being addressed and clarify that the four interconnected dimensions of historical thinking are (1) chronological thinking, (2) historical comprehension, (3) historical analysis

Table C.1: Vocabulary to Preteach

Tier One	Tier Two	Tier Three
concrete	critical thinking	rhetorical flourish
building blocks	realities	philosophy
content	context	fetishism
	developing	sophism
	aim	Montaigne
	central	
	human condition	
	just	
	depend on	
	ground	
	facility	
	associated with	

and interpretation, and (4) historical research. The objective is to understand and apply the process historians use to explain the history of North Carolina, the United States, and the world.

Focus on the first paragraph of "Critical Thinking: A Lesson From the Past on What Matters."

> The Social Sciences aim at developing critical thinking about issues and ideas central to the human condition. *This sentence is very long. I will chunk it to help me understand it.* The Social Sciences—*Hmm, that must be like social studies*—aim at developing critical thinking—*So, this tells me that the aim or goal of social studies is to build critical thinking. I remember my teacher said that critical thinking is when we analyze and assess what we hear and read*—about issues and ideas central to the human condition—*in other words on aspects of existing as a human.*
>
> Just as our verbal skills—*our speaking abilities*—depend upon words as building blocks, facts provide the vocabulary—*facts are like the building blocks or tools*—that grounds our writing and thinking—*that make our writing and thinking firm or strong*—in concrete, common understandable realities—*in other words in real life. So, I'll reread this to put it all together.*

Reread the entire passage and close with a summary, such as the following.

> *OK, so the writer is using an analogy to clarify. He compares words used in conversations or discussions to facts used in writing and thinking about social sciences.*

Partner Reading With Summary

(Ten to fifteen minutes)

Split the teams into pairs, and have them read paragraphs two to five as partners. They then summarize what they've read using sentence starters such as:

- "This passage is mostly about . . ."
- "This passage discusses, describes, explains, or supports . . ."

After-Reading Strategy

(Twenty or more minutes)

In teams, students create a graphic organizer depicting the critical thinking that should occur in historical analysis. The graphic organizer should show the relationship of these words: *fact, judgment, interpretation,* and *action.* Teams can add other words as needed.

Teams then write two to three questions following Bloom's Taxonomy that other teams will answer to show their understanding of the graphic.

Once the graphic organizers and questions are complete, post them in the classroom. In a gallery walk, students review the graphic organizers and post responses to the questions.

Writing Strategies

For brief writing, students can use an exit pass to write two or three sentences, analyzing and assessing an idea in the reading.

For longer writing, have students use the strategy *write around.* Teams of four write an essay and use evidence from the text and online sources, such as a newspaper clipping, to think critically about the topic in question.

Performance Assessments

Vocabulary: Evidence of students using the targeted vocabulary in step 6 of the seven steps of preteaching vocabulary and in their summaries

Reading: Evidence of students' ability to provide an accurate summary of the text distinct from prior knowledge or opinions, which the teacher collects as she circulates and listens to partners summarize during paired reading (RH.9–10.2)

Writing: Exit pass (WHST.9–10.2)

Content knowledge: Partner summaries and graphic organizers that show understanding of critical thinking in historical analysis and an exit pass that shows ability to apply critical thinking to a reading

Teacher Reflection

ExC-ELL Observation Protocol indicators for this lesson include the following.

- **3.0–3.7:** Uses the seven steps (see chapter 2) to teach the words or phrasal clusters selected

- **4.1:** Builds content and vocabulary background for students from different cultural and educational experiences

- **4.3:** Models using think-alouds to teach comprehension strategies specific to that text before students read

- **4.4:** Requires students to practice the specific comprehension strategy just modeled

- **4.5:** Requires partner reading and partner summaries using key vocabulary (tier two and tier three); monitors and records individual skills applied

- **4.6:** Models sentence starters and phrasal clusters to be used for their peer summaries and whole-class discussions

The teacher notes which content standards have been met and which vocabulary words or clusters, reading strategies, and writing skills need further work. The teacher may note these on the student application side of the ExC-ELL Observation Protocol.

Following this reflection, the teacher has students do the following.

- Teams review and respond to questions from the gallery walk.

- Using their graphic organizers, students craft questions to ask themselves or a partner as they think critically on a historical topic. Examples might be:

    - How does the author know this?

    - Why did this occur?

    - Which evidence is most believable?

- Students organize questions under the headings on the graphic organizer they created.

- If students would like to finish the reading, stronger readers can complete the reading through partner reading with summary while other students research the writers, places, and people the article references. Teachers can have students use a jigsaw to research these people and places and then share their findings with the whole group. Likewise, students completing the reading of "Critical Thinking: A Lesson From the Past on What Matters" should share their summaries with the whole class. Students then adjust their graphic organizers and crafted questions as necessary.

SAMPLE MATHEMATICS LESSON: RATIOS AND PROPORTIONAL RELATIONSHIPS

By Maria Trejo

Timing: This lesson may take several days depending on the depth and number of lessons the teacher presents.

Subject: Mathematics

Title of mentor text and ancillary materials: District assigned textbooks and materials; CCSS for mathematics; local-district-adopted standards

Content Standards

Use ratios and proportional relationships to solve real-world and mathematical problems using numerical and algebraic equations.

Common Core State Standards for Mathematics, Ratios and Proportional Relationships

7.RP.A.1: Compute unit rates associated with ratios of fractions, including ratios of lengths, areas and other quantities measured in like or different units.

7.RP.A.2: Recognize and represent proportional relationships between quantities.

7.RP.A.3: Use proportional relationships to solve multistep ratio and percent problems. (NGA & CCSSO, 2010c)

English Language Development Standards

Standard 3: Students at all levels of English language proficiency interact with grade-level words, and expressions to integrate and evaluate content presented in diverse formats and media. They use ratio language and information necessary to describe relationships between quantities and to solve math problems that involve ratios and proportions (WIDA, 2012, p. 90).

Sample Problems

Following are two problems using the Common Core standard 7.RP.A.3, "Use proportional relationships to solve multistep ratio and percent problems" (NGA & CCSSO, 2010c).

1. **The teacher provides a word problem to illustrate the lesson:** Pedro makes $25.00 an hour, and he gets a $2.50 raise. He would like to know what part to whole is the additional raise in fractions or percentage.

2. **The students practice solving a similar word problem to see if they understood the preliminary instructions and mathematical procedures:** Phil wants to place a towel bar 9¾ inches long in the center of a door that is 27½ inches wide, and he estimates that he will need to place the bar about 9 inches from each edge. Confirm or deny his estimate, and determine the exact computation.

Preteaching Vocabulary and Disclosure

(Twelve minutes)

Preteach five to six targeted words or clusters per reading segment that are key to comprehension, discussions, and text-based writing. We've identified vocabulary from both sample problems. See table D.1.

Table D.1: Vocabulary to Preteach

Tier One	Tier Two	Tier Three
raise	center of	ratio
additional	from each edge	rate
about	estimate	fraction bar
check	compare	colon
towel bar	quantity	equivalent
	relationship	computation
		part to whole

Methods and Procedures

Restate the objective of the lesson:

You will understand the concept of a ratio and use ratio language to describe relationships between quantities. You will also learn that ratios may be expressed in three ways: a part to a whole, a whole to a part, and part of a whole to another part, or a rate to a rate. The language of ratios may also be expressed in three ways: with the word **to***, with a colon (:), or by a fraction or fraction bar (½).*

Review key vocabulary and phrases using the seven-step vocabulary process (see chapter 2, page 35). Selected vocabulary for the first lesson may be *part to whole*, *estimate*, and *additional*.

See table D.2 for an example of the process with one phrase: *part to whole*.

Introduce mathematical concepts and procedures to solve problems using ratios and proportions. For the following team-building activities, form heterogeneous teams of three or four students, mixing English learners and native English speakers. Ask each team to discuss the sample problems, key vocabulary, and procedures for solving the problems (three to five minutes). You could also have students use the following discourse strategies.

- Teams of three or four

- Partners

- Whole-class response

- Partner reading

Table D.2: Seven Steps for Preteaching Vocabulary

Step	Example
1. Teacher says the word or phrase and asks students to repeat it three times.	"Repeat after me, *part to whole, part to whole, part to whole*."
2. Teacher states the word in context from the text.	"He would like to know what *part to whole* is . . ."
3. Teacher provides the dictionary definition.	"A ratio is a proportion or the relationship of a *part to whole* number."

continued >

Step	Example
4. Teacher provides the student-friendly definition.	"We express *parts of* something in relationship to a *whole*. For example, for every dollar there are four quarters. So, every quarter is one-fourth of a dollar or twenty-five cents is one-fourth of a dollar."
5. Teacher highlights features of the word: polysemous meanings, cognate, tense, prefixes, and so on.	"*Part* is a polysemous word because it has a different meaning in different uses, as in 'She parted with her doll willingly.' (She gave it up or let it go.) 'They parted ways as friends.' (They left each other.) 'He took part in it for three days last year.' (He participated in it.) It is also a cognate of *parte* or *partir*. *Part* can also be used as a verb, and then it means to cut up or to divide, as in 'He parted the watermelon in six pieces.'"
6. Teacher engages all students in activities to develop word or concept knowledge.	"Turn to your buddy, and share a statement using the concept *part to whole* in a mathematics sentence. Each one of you will share three examples, such as 'I am one part of a whole family,' 'One inch is part of a whole foot,' or 'Monday is part of a whole week.'"
7. Teacher reminds students when to use the word.	"Remember that *part of something*, *part to whole*, *a ratio*, and a *portion of* all refer to the same concept. Remember to use these phrases when you develop your word problems."

Teacher Read-Aloud, Think-Aloud

(Twenty minutes)

Provide support and opportunities for guided practice of new mathematics skills and vocabulary with the use of a read-aloud, a think-aloud, or partner reading. Model close-reading strategies of rereading, self-correction, questioning, anticipating steps to solving the problems, and identifying new or troublesome vocabulary. Tell students whenever you incorporate selected domains of the CCSS for mathematics. Use the eight Standards for Mathematical Practice (NGA & CCSSO, 2010c).

1. Make sense of problems and persevere in solving them.

2. Reason abstractly and quantitatively.

3. Construct viable arguments and critique the reasoning of others.

4. Model with mathematics.

5. Use appropriate tools strategically.

6. Attend to precision.

7. Look for and make use of structure.

8. Look for and express regularity in repeated reasoning.

Begin by reading the problem and adding in your thought process:

Phil wants to place a towel bar 9¾ inches long in the center of a door that is 27½ inches wide, and he estimates that he will need to place the bar about

9 inches from each edge. Confirm or deny his estimate and determine the exact computation.

Let's see, I'm thinking about questioning, *and* anticipating steps to solving problems. *So, what the problem is asking me to do is to verify or check that the 9-inch estimate is correct. One way to solve the problem will be to draw a picture of a door that represents 27½ inches, find the middle of the door, or divide 27½ by 2. Then, I will do the same for the towel bar. Divide 9½ by half. I will then align both halves and then measure the difference of both end points. I'll try this first and then check to see if I am approximately 9 inches from each edge of the door.*

Have students practice thinking aloud and then practice the oral strategies while thinking of other ways to solve the problem. For example:

I will also draw a door to help me see if my answer makes sense. But I think that I can solve the problem using round numbers to estimate where the bar would be placed. I will think of 27½ as 28 and divide that in half to give me 14. Then, I will think of 9¾ as 10 and divide that in half to give me 5. Is 9 the difference between 14 and 5 or close to it? Yes. Therefore, I know that my thinking is correct.

Partner Reading With Summary

(Ten to fifteen minutes)

Model partner reading. If the word problems are too short, partner reading is done one whole problem at a time. Student A reads the problem, Student B helps clarify issues or summarizes what is being asked, Student A starts making suggestions on needed steps to solve the problem, and Student B helps.

Direct students to pair up and use the same strategies. Remind them to also look for and read text structures, such as instructions, graphs, charts, and keys in the text.

Students read and discuss the problems first and then proceed to outline steps to solve each problem. Students may continue to work in pairs, triads, or groups of four, depending on the number of problems or complexity of the projects.

Class Debrief Strategy

(Fifteen minutes)

After students have had an opportunity to practice reading and solving problems, use Numbered Heads Together with guided questions and prompts to help students solidify their understanding. Following are examples of guided questions and prompts.

- What is a ratio, and what are the different ways to express ratios (in words or symbols)?

- Share two examples of how the concept of ratios is used in everyday life.

- Why do we need to use ratios?
- How does a chef use ratios? How does an architect use ratios? Give examples of how other professions use the concept of part to whole.

Group students in fours, and have them number off one to four. Read a question, and direct team members to put their heads together, discuss the answer, and ensure that each member understands the question and knows the answer. Call a number; students with that number stand up. Each student standing provides an answer to the question. Other students help, if necessary. You decide if each answer is right or not. The process continues until all students standing up have answered the question.

Feel free to modify this strategy to make it a game or a competition, allocating points to each team that answers correctly.

Four Corners Strategy

(Fifteen minutes)

Ask students to number themselves from one to four. Students then go to the designated four corners of the room based on their number. The teacher asks students to form triads within each group. Assign any extra students at each corner to form a new group; it's OK if a group has two or four students. Teachers can expedite this process by posting the numbers in the corners.

To ensure that all students participate, tell students that each of them can only speak for thirty seconds. Ask one of the groups a question, such as "What profession or life situation uses ratios, and how are they used?" A student from that group answers the question, the next student clarifies or adds to the answer, and the next student does the same. Repeat the question with a different group. Afterward, ask one or two students to share responses with the class. This gives you the opportunity to clarify or ask students for more information. The process continues until you interact with all groups.

Placemat Strategy

(Ten minutes)

Direct students to mark and divide a piece of paper in three or four large sections using markers. Each student needs to have a designated section or placemat to contribute his work.

Instruct students to solve one of the problems given to their group. They discuss the problem as a group, then each student—in his or her respective section of the paper—writes steps to solve the problem, and writes a solution, starting at the top of the section so as to leave space for others to continue working on the same section.

This process allows for all students to participate, to solve problems using a variety of strategies, and to learn from each other's thinking.

When all students finish one answer, they hand the paper to the student in their group on their right. All students read what their neighbors wrote. They then review their neighbors' steps and answers. Students continue to write new answers and strategies immediately under the previous students'. The process continues until the group answers all problems.

At the end of the writing process, students discuss the various answers, personal perspectives, new ideas, or new questions that they may have generated during the discussions. The teacher then may select a student to share ideas generated at their respective tables.

Writing Strategies

(Twenty minutes)

After students have learned and practiced solving word problems involving the concept of ratios, complete the following three steps.

1. Each student drafts a word problem that includes ratios and steps to solve the problem.

2. Students read all of the word problems they drafted and select a problem to refine and solve with their designated partners. Teachers can use problems students don't select for a similar activity later.

3. In pairs or triads, students edit, read, and solve the word problems they drafted, using the Cut and Grow strategy.

    a. Read and edit the wording of the problem, if necessary for clarification.

    b. Write a way or process to solve the problem.

    c. Explain and defend the answer.

    d. Instead of erasing or deleting what has been entered so far, cut the paper at the end of the first solution or steps; then paste a different color paper to provide clean space to add an alternative process for solving the problem. Edit the problem's wording if it needs further clarification, and write an alternative way or process to solve the problem.

    e. Defend your answer and various ways to solving the problem.

Students can repeat the process two to four times, depending on the complexity or the possible ways to solve the problem.

Performance Assessments

Vocabulary: Exit passes that show understanding of a key word, its equivalent symbol, and definition in students' own words, with graphics as necessary

Reading: Evidence of students' abilities during paired reading

Writing: Cut and Grow pages that show successful problem creation

Content knowledge: Accurate oral discussions and student explanations

Teacher Reflection

ExC-ELL Observation Protocol indicators for this lesson include the following.

- **1.1–1.4:** Models high classroom-management skills
- **2.1–2.5:** Incorporates a variety of cooperative learning strategies
- **3.0–3.7:** Uses the seven steps to teach key words and concepts
- **4.2, 4.3, 4.5:** Uses selected reading strategies, as appropriate
- **6.1, 6.2, 6.5, 6.6:** Uses selected writing strategies to solidify understanding of new vocabulary and concepts
- **7.1–7.6:** Uses instructional strategies to ensure that students are addressing the eight Standards for Mathematical Practice

Note whether students have met the content standards and which vocabulary words or clusters, reading strategies, and writing skills need further work. Reflect on student collaboration skills.

SAMPLE SCIENCE LESSON: CONSUMPTION OF NATURAL RESOURCES

By Maria Trejo

Timing: This lesson will take three or four class periods, depending on how extensively students research the topic.

Subject: Science (grades 9 to 12), earth and human activity

Title of mentor text and ancillary materials: *Human Migration and Global Change: Why Are People Moving Around? Does It Matter?* by Joy Kreeft Peyton (2013)

Content Standards

Next Generation Science Standards

Standard (MS-ESS3-4): Students will demonstrate understanding of how increases in human population per-capita consumption of natural resources affects the Earth's systems by constructing an argument supported by evidence.

Disciplinary Core Idea (ESS3.C): Typically as human populations and per-capita consumption of natural resources increase, so do the negative impacts on the Earth, unless the activities and technologies involved are engineered otherwise.

Science and Engineering Practices (MS-ESS3-4): Students will construct an oral and written argument supported by empirical evidence and scientific reasoning to support or refute an explanation related to the impact of population migration and growth. (NGSS Lead States, 2013)

Students will use the crosscutting concept of cause and effect relationships to predict short- and long-term consequences of population and migration and growth.

Core questions to study include:

- How do increases in human population per-capita consumption of natural resources affect the Earth's systems?

- How can science, engineering, and technology help us understand the impact of future migration and population growth in the United States?

Common Core State Standards

RL.5.1: Quote accurately from a text when explaining what the text says explicitly and when drawing inferences from the text.

RI.5.2: Determine two or more main ideas of a text and explain how they are supported by key details; summarize the text.

W.5.9: Draw evidence from informational texts, Internet, and periodicals to support analysis, reflection, and research. (NGA & CCSSO, 2010a)

English Language Development Standards

Standard 4: Integrate and evaluate content presented in diverse formats and media, including visually and quantitatively, as well as in words. Write arguments to support claims in an analysis of substantive topics or texts using valid reasoning and relevant and sufficient evidence. (WIDA, 2012, p. 20)

Preteaching Vocabulary and Discourse

(Twelve minutes)

Preteach five to six targeted words or clusters per reading segment that are key to reading comprehension, discussions, and text-based writing. See table E.1.

Table E.1: Vocabulary to Preteach

Tier One	Tier Two	Tier Three
resources	to integrate	sustainable places
voluntarily	migrating people	sustainable lifestyles
involuntarily	life-giving opportunities	scarce resources
challenges	lead to	within countries
desirable	as the impact	across countries
	to ensure	asylee
	due to	
	since	

Methods and Procedures

Introduce the topic and the purpose of the lesson by stating the purpose of the lesson:

> *You are going to be studying how increases in human population have an impact on the Earth's systems and constructing an argument supported by evidence. You will look at both positive and negative impacts by researching texts, searching the Internet, reviewing periodicals, and interviewing community leaders or family members.*

Review key vocabulary and phrases using the seven-step vocabulary process (see chapter 2, page 35). Table E.2 shows an example of the process with *sustainable*.

Table E.2: Seven Steps for Preteaching Vocabulary

Step	Example
1. Teacher says the word or phrase and asks students to repeat it three times.	"Repeat after me, *sustainable, sustainable, sustainable.*"
2. Teacher states the word in context from the text.	"If the people migrate involuntarily, and the receiving community accepts them and finds *sustainable* places for them to live, their experience in the new place can be wonderful."
3. Teacher provides the dictionary definition.	"To *sustain* is to keep from failing during duress or difficulty."
4. Teacher provides the student-friendly definition.	"It also means to support, to uphold, or to prove."
5. The teacher highlights features of the word: polysemous meanings, cognate, tense, prefixes, and so on.	"*Sostener* is the Spanish cognate. *Sustainable* is a polysemous word when it means *to prove* ('The testimony *sustained* the evidence') or *to prolong* ('She *sustained* the high tones in the song for a long time')."
6. Teacher engages students in activities to develop word or concept knowledge.	"Talk with a buddy at your table. Using the word *sustainable* or *sustain*, give examples of how it has applied to a personal situation. For example, 'He thought that I had left him behind, but I did not. I *sustained* my innocence.' or 'If someone decides to go on a diet, it is a good idea to select one that is *sustainable*.'"
7. Teacher reminds students when to use the word.	"As you do your research, remember to use these words and *sustain* your conclusions."

Teacher Read-Aloud, Think-Aloud

(Twenty minutes)

Begin by reading the problem and stating your focus.

> *I must remember that I will be reading to answer the question, "What happens when people migrate?"*

> If the people migrate involuntarily (because of war, political or religious oppression or persecution, or climate challenges)—*yes, I know of people who have left their countries because of wars*—and the receiving community accepts them and finds sustainable places—*I know that this means places where they can live over a period of time*—for them in the community, their experience in the new place can be a wonderful, life-giving opportunity for them.

Students practice reading and thinking aloud with a partner at their table. Teachers remind them to take turns reading a paragraph each and summarizing at the end of each sentence. When they finish reading a section from the mentor text, they summarize key points:

> *We need to know much more about what happens when large numbers of people move from one country to the next. And we need to learn what happens to both the country they leave behind and the new one.*

Elbow Buddy Summary Strategy

(Five minutes)

Have students turn to their elbow buddies and discuss the following: "Did your family or ancestors emigrate from another country? Do you have examples of how immigrant populations have had an impact in your state or city? Think of impacts that you perceive as positive and negative in heath, technology, water, education, arts, music, or others."

Scientific Inquiry Questions Strategy

(Twelve minutes)

Organize students into research teams of four. Instruct each group to select a passage to read and research regarding the topic. Areas to study might include the impact of immigrants on health services, educational services, urban planning, or the prison system. Once each group has selected an area, model open-ended questions to prepare for the research. Provide an example, such as the following:

> *What do we know about human migration? Some people say that new immigrants take resources from local residents. Could this be true? Why is this topic important to us? What other subjects are we studying that relate to this topic?*

What are two big ideas that we want to research? What are the benefits and the disadvantages of immigrant populations in a specific location?

Students formulate a few more questions or subcategories of questions related to the topic. They then decide who in the group is going to research which question.

Journal Writing and Inquiry Theory Development

(Ten minutes)

Model how to rewrite preproject inquiry questions. Say something like:

Students, remember that in the area of science we do not guess at information, and we do not state personal opinions about topics that we research. We must look for evidence to maintain our positions. This process requires us to write our questions in nonbiased and neutral inquiry statements. Let's take a statement such as "I think that too many immigrants is a problem because they increase traffic congestion, they crowd our schools, and they do not contribute much." First, we need to separate all the various concerns referenced in the statement, and then we need write smaller questions as inquiries that we want to know more about and come to a conclusion that is supported by evidence.

Students work in their groups of four to formulate their questions.

Reading and Research Activities

(Twenty minutes)

Direct students to read the section, "Are there ways to ensure that national and international migration is successful and beneficial?" (Peyton, 2013, pp. 3–4). Their assignment is to read with their partners and see if any of their questions can be answered by this document.

Each group discusses what it has read. Students may decide that they have found some answers but not enough to sustain their information. They then identify what needs further investigation.

A student from each group shares with the whole class key points or statements from the text that begin to answer some of the questions and questions that need further research. For example, the class may decide that there is not enough information in the mentor text to answer the question, "Do immigrants increase traffic congestion?"

Direct students to study their original inquiry questions to see if they need to rewrite them before beginning the next phase of their research. Invite the group to list resources where students might find the answers, such as the library, the Internet, or periodicals.

Research Questions

(Twenty minutes)

Students enter key points and data in their journals from their research. They also continue to reformulate questions. For example, a student might write, "In the mentor text, the author stated that one reason that people migrate from one place to the next is that the climate they live in becomes intolerable, and they must seek better climate and living conditions. If this is true, I would like to find out where the largest population of immigrants to the United States comes from and see if climate has anything to do with their decision to move."

Have students research using books, periodicals, and the Internet and ask community leaders or family members to share their experiences with immigrants and their impact on life in their state, city, community, or school.

First Draft Strategy

(Five minutes)

Model using cause and effect to prepare students for writing their preliminary findings. Explain to the class that scientists often use cause-and-effect words to accurately record the reason for something happening, such as *because, when, since, consequently,* and *due to.*

Remind students that cause-and-effect words help the writer organize information and positions. They indicate an event that happened (its effect) as a result of something (its cause). Common examples would be "If you practice hard, your skills will improve. When you overeat, your stomach hurts."

Refer students to the mentor text to find examples where the author uses these words (Peyton, 2013).

Observation Notes

(Five minutes)

Remind students to think like a scientist when writing preliminary notes or statements about cause and effect. Scientists use caution in reporting research by using words and phrases such as *it appears, I read, I observed, appears to be, it seems that,* and *one explanation may be.*

Have students practice using the transition words with their elbow buddies. They may say something like "It seems that when more people move into a town, the traffic increases, but I am not sure how many people it takes to create traffic jams."

Write Around Activity

(Twenty minutes)

In small groups, students write three paragraphs about a topic. All students complete a sentence fragment you give them, such as "Immigrant populations have the potential to have a positive or negative impact on their new country if . . ." Each student writes one sentence and passes the paper to the right. The receiving student reads the narrative and adds one more sentence. Ask students to use the cause-and-effect format and vocabulary words or phrases when making statements.

After students write three paragraphs, have students revise content closely and check for overgeneralizations, lack of facts, wrong references, and missing key information. Next, they edit grammar, delete repetitions, fix incomplete sentences, rethink titles, and ensure that they have a strong ending that answers the question they're studying. Students can complete this activity in a couple of class periods or longer, depending on how deeply you want students to investigate the topic.

Performance Assessments

Vocabulary: Evidence in student journals of key inquiry questions using tier two words

Reading: Evidence of understanding during think-alouds, read-alouds, and paired reading

Writing: Evidence of understanding in students' written work

Content knowledge: Correct answers on quizzes in science texts

Teacher Reflection

ExC-ELL Observation Protocol indicators for this lesson include the following.

- **3.0–3.7:** Uses the seven steps to teach these words, clusters, and phrases: *to integrate, migrating people, life-giving opportunities, lead to, as the impact,* and *to ensure*

- **4.1:** Builds content and vocabulary background for students from different cultural backgrounds and with different migration and educational experiences

- **4.3:** Models using think-alouds to teach comprehension strategies specific to the text before students read

- **4.4:** Requires students to practice the specific comprehension strategy just modeled

- **4.5:** Requires partner reading and partner summaries using key vocabulary (tier two and tier three) and monitors and records individual skills applied

- **4.6:** Models sentence starters and phrasal clusters to be used for peer summaries and whole-class discussions

- **4.7:** Engages students in academic discussions using text-dependent questions that require evidence from text

- **6.1:** Expects text-dependent writing

- **6.6:** Uses revision strategies (open-ended questions, journal writing, inquiry theory development, cause-and-effect format, use of scientific words, and the three-part writing process)

- **6.7:** Uses editing strategies (open-ended questions, journal writing, inquiry theory development, cause-and-effect format, use of scientific words, and the three-part writing process)

Make observations each time students use a strategy, and debrief their work. During the debriefing and student discussions, make note of the use of new vocabulary, information referenced or quoted, and student observations and conclusions. Begin and end the class period by restating the standard and key questions under study.

APPENDIX F

SAMPLE LESSON TEMPLATE

Teachers should sequentially distribute the key features of instruction from oracy to reading to writing, using many instructional strategies for each. The way to integrate these features into an active teaching repertoire consists of a set of whole-school action plans that include a comprehensive three- to five-day initial institute for teachers, follow-up onsite modeling, observations, and coaching for trained teachers; establishment of collegial learning through onsite small communities of practice or online networks to review lesson components, share lessons, and answer questions; and tools to gauge teaching and learning growth and impact.

Following is a lesson-plan template for teachers or teams of teachers that zooms in on the fidelity, frequency, and quality of instruction and on how students respond to that instruction. It also includes a final section for teacher reflection.

ExC-ELL Lesson-Plan Template

Teacher: _____

Subject: _____

Date: _____

Title of Mentor Text and Ancillary Materials: _____

State or Common Core State Standard: _____

English Language Development Standards: _____

Preteaching Vocabulary and Discourse

Select targeted words and word clusters from text necessary for reading comprehension, discussions, and text-based writing. Use twelve minutes to preteach five or six of these words. You can teach others during or after reading. Highlight the ones you want to see in students' writing.

Tier One	Tier Two	Tier Three

Methods and Procedures

Team Formation and Team-Building Activities

Discourse strategies throughout the lesson (four corners, clock buddies, circle of friends, and so on):

Teacher read-aloud, think-aloud to model strategy students need to use:

Partner reading with summary (page _____):

Student reading approach after partner reading (page _____):

Choral reading (page _____):

Silent reading with buddy summaries (page _____):

After-reading strategy to anchor knowledge, language, and literacy (question formulation, Numbered Heads Together, roundtable, graphic organizer, team presentation, jigsaws, and so on; pages _____):

Writing strategies for drafting, revising, editing, and publishing (page _____):

Performance Assessments

Vocabulary: _____

Reading: _____

Writing: _____

Content knowledge: _____

Teacher Reflection

Targeted ExC-ELL Observation Protocol indicators:

Reflection (may include coach or teacher learning community):

Next steps:

Page 2 of 2

REFERENCES AND RESOURCES

Achievement Strategies. (n.d.). *Summary templates*. Accessed at www.achievementstrategies.org /summaryTemplates.html on August 31, 2015.

Adams, J. M. (2013). *Social and emotional learning gaining new focus under Common Core*. Accessed at http://edsource.org/2013/social-and-emotional-learning-gaining-new-traction-under -commoncore/32161 on August 7, 2015.

AdLit.org. (2015). *Classroom strategies: Text structure*. Accessed at www.adlit.org/strategies/23336 /monitor their comprehension on May 13, 2015.

Alliance for Excellent Education. (2012). *The role of language and literacy in college- and career-ready standards: Rethinking policy and practice in support of English language learners*. Accessed at www .marylandpublicschools.org/cc/12.pdf on May 19, 2015.

Allington, R. L. (2001). *What really matters for struggling readers: Designing research-based programs*. New York: Longman.

Allington, R. L. (2014). *The six Ts of effective elementary literacy instruction*. Accessed at www .readingrockets.org/article/96 on February 13, 2015.

Anderson, L. W., & Krathwohl, D. R. (Eds.). (2001). *A taxonomy for learning, teaching and assessing: A revision of Bloom's taxonomy of educational objectives* (Complete ed.). New York: Longman.

August, D., & Hakuta, K. (Eds.). (1998). *Educating language-minority children*. Washington, DC: National Academies Press. Accessed at www.nap.edu/openbook.php?record_id=6025 on February 13, 2015.

August, D., & Shanahan, T. (Eds.). (2006). *Developing literacy in second language learners: Report of the National Literacy Panel on Language Minority Children and Youth*. Mahwah, NJ: Erlbaum.

August, D., & Shanahan, T. (Eds.). (2008). *Developing reading and writing in second-language learners: Lessons from the report of the National Literacy Panel on Language Minority Children and Youth*. New York: Routledge.

Austin Independent School District. (n.d.). *Summary of informational-expository text*. Accessed at http://curriculum.austinisd.org/la/resources/documents/2012–2013Informational -ExpositorySummaryORSModule.pdf on February 17, 2015.

Austin Independent School District. (2013). *Summary of narrative text*. Accessed at http:// curriculum.austinisd.org/la/resources/documents/NarrativeSummaryORSModule1213.pdf on February 17, 2015.

Baker, F. W. (n.d.). *Informational text features*. Accessed at www.frankwbaker.com/what_are _informational_texts.htm on May 13, 2015.

Biemiller, A. (2011). Vocabulary: What words should we teach? *Better: Evidence-Based Education*, *3*(2), 10–11. Accessed at www.betterevidence.org/uk-edition/issue-6/vocabulary-what-words -should-we-teach on February 13, 2015.

Bransford, J., Brown, A., & Cocking, R. (Eds.). (2000). *How people learn: Brain, mind, experience, and school* (Expanded ed.). Washington, DC: National Academies Press. Accessed at www.csun .edu/~SB4310/How%20People%20Learn.pdf on February 13, 2015.

Bridgeland, J. M., Dilulio, J. J., & Morison, K. B. (2006). *The silent epidemic: Perspectives of high school dropouts*. Washington, DC: Civic Enterprises.

Calderón, M. (2007). *Teaching reading to English language learners, grades 6–12: A framework for improving achievement in the content areas*. Thousand Oaks, CA: Corwin Press.

Calderón, M. (2009). Language, literacy and knowledge for ELLs. *Better: Evidence-Based Education*, *1*(1), 14–15. Accessed at www.betterevidence.org/us-edition/issue-1/language-literacy-and -knowledge-for-ells on February 13, 2015.

Calderón, M. (2011a). *Teaching reading and comprehension to English language learners, K–5*. Bloomington, IN: Solution Tree Press.

Calderón, M. (2011b). Teaching writing to ELLs in high schools. *Better: Evidence-Based Education*, *3*(2), 8–9. Accessed at http://esl.ncwiseowl.org/UserFiles/Servers/Server_4502383/File/all.pdf on February 13, 2015.

Calderón, M. (Ed.). (2012). *Breaking through: Effective instruction and assessment for reaching English learners*. Bloomington, IN: Solution Tree Press.

Calderón, M. (2013). *ExC-ELL observation protocol (EOP): Expediting comprehension for English language learners*. Washington, DC: Author.

Calderón, M., Carreón, A., Cantú, J., & Minaya-Rowe, L. (2010). *Expediting comprehension for English language learners: Participants' manual*. New York: Benchmark Education.

Calderón, M., Carreón, A., Cantú, J., & Minaya-Rowe, L. (2012). *Expediting comprehension for English language learners: Participants' manual*. New York: Benchmark Education.

Calderón, M. E., Carreón, A., Peyton, J. K., & Slakk, S. (2015). *ExC-ELL: Expediting comprehension for English language learners—Participants' manual*. New Rochelle, NY: Benchmark Education Co.

Calderón, M., Hertz-Lazarowitz, R., & Slavin, R. E. (1998). Effects of bilingual cooperative integrated reading and composition on students making the transition from Spanish to English reading. *The Elementary School Journal*, *99*(2), 153–165.

Calderón, M. E., & Minaya-Rowe, L. (2011). *Preventing long-term ELs: Transforming schools to meet core standards*. Thousand Oaks, CA: Corwin Press.

Calderón, M. E., Minaya-Rowe, L., Carreón, A., Durán, D., & Fitch, A. (2009). *Preparing teachers of math, science and social studies with English language learners: A report to the Carnegie Corporation of New York*. New York: Carnegie.

Calderón, M. E., Slavin, R. E., & Sánchez, M. (2011). Effective instruction for English language learners. In M. Tienda & R. Haskins (Eds.), *The future of immigrant children* (pp. 103–128). Washington, DC: Brookings Institute/Princeton University.

California Department of Education. (2012). *California English language development (ELD) standards.* Accessed at www.cde.ca.gov/sp/el/er/eldstandards.asp on February 13, 2015.

California Department of Education. (2013a). *California Common Core State Standards: English language arts and literacy in history / social studies, science, and technical subjects.* Accessed at www.cde.ca.gov/be/st/ss/documents/finalelaccssstandards.pdf on February 17, 2015.

California Department of Education. (2013b). *California Common Core State Standards: Mathematics.* Accessed at www.cde.ca.gov/be/st/ss/documents/ccssmathstandardaug2013.pdf on February 13, 2015.

California Department of Education. (2013c). *Mathematics framework for California Public Schools, kindergarten through grade twelve: Appendix D—Sample mathematics problems.* Accessed at www.cde.ca.gov/ci/ma/cf/documents/aug2013apxdmathmodel.pdf on July 17, 2015.

Capital One Financial Corporation. (2010). *Capital One's annual back-to-school shopping survey reveals gap in back-to-school budget expectations between parents, teens* [Press release]. Accessed at http://press.capitalone.com/phoenix.zhtml%3Fc%3D251626%26p%3Dirol-newsArticle%26ID%3D1858699%26highlight%3D on September 22, 2015.

Chamot, A. U., & O'Malley, J. M. (1994). *The CALLA handbook: Implementing the cognitive academic language learning approach.* New York: Addison-Wesley.

Chicago Public Schools. (2012). *CCSS and SEL in the Chicago public schools* [PowerPoint]. Accessed at https://casel.squarespace.com/s/FRI-13-Cheatham-CPS-CCSS-SEL.ppt on July 28, 2015.

Cogan, L. S., Schmidt, W. H., & Wiley, D. E. (2001). Who takes what math and in which track? Using TIMSS to characterize U.S. students' eighth-grade mathematics learning opportunities. *Educational Evaluation and Policy Analysis, 23*(4), 323–341.

Coleman, D., & Pimentel, S. (2012). *Revised publishers' criteria for the Common Core State Standards in English language arts and literacy, grades 3–12.* Washington, DC: Council of Chief State School Officers. Accessed at http://165.74.253.64/be/cc/cd/documents/sept2012item2aatt3.pdf on February 13, 2015.

Collaborative for Academic, Social, and Emotional Learning. (2003). *Safe and sound: An educational leader's guide to evidence-based social and emotional learning (SEL) programs.* Chicago: Author.

Collaborative for Academic, Social, and Emotional Learning. (2012). *Frequently asked questions about social and emotional learning (SEL).* Chicago: Author.

Collaborative for Academic, Social, and Emotional Learning. (2013). *CASEL schoolkit: A guide for implementing schoolwide academic, social, and emotional learning.* Unpublished manuscript, Collaborative for Academic, Social, and Emotional Learning, Chicago.

Collaborative for Academic, Social, and Emotional Learning. (2014). *Guide for Schoolwide Social & Emotional Learning.* Unpublished manuscript, Collaborative for Academic, Social and Emotional Learning, Chicago.

Committee on the Study of Teacher Preparation Programs in the United States. (2010). *Preparing teachers: Building evidence for sound policy.* Washington, DC: National Research Council.

Crawford-Brooke, E. (2013). *The critical role of oral language in reading for Title I students and English language learners.* Accessed at http://lexialearning.com/lexiaresearch/whitepapers /oral-language-whitepaper on February 13, 2015.

Cummins, J. (1981). The role of primary language development in promoting educational success for language minority students. In California State Department of Education (Ed.), *Schooling and language minority students: A theoretical framework* (pp. 3–50). Los Angeles: California State University.

Cummins, J. (2012). Whole-school approaches to academic language proficiency among English learners. In M. Calderón (Ed.), *Breaking through: Effective instruction and assessment for reaching English learners* (pp. 63–88). Bloomington, IN: Solution Tree Press.

Czarnecki, J. G. (2001). *Summary checklists for different text structures.* Accessed at www.thinkport .org/73bec609-f1cd-427f-8602-c632b4d0bb74.asset on February 13, 2015.

Darling-Hammond, L. (2003). Standards and assessments: Where we are and what we need. *Teachers College Record.* Accessed at www.tcrecord.org/content.asp?contentid=11109 on May 22, 2015.

Devaney, E., O'Brien, M. U., Resnik, H., Keister, S., & Weissberg, R. P. (2006). *Sustainable schoolwide social and emotional learning (SEL): Implementation guide and toolkit.* Chicago: Collaborative for Academic, Social, and Emotional Learning.

Donovan, M. S., & Bransford, J. D. (Eds.). (2005). *How students learn: History, mathematics, and science in the classroom.* Washington, DC: The National Academies.

DuFour, R., DuFour, R., Eaker, R., & Karhanek, G. (2010). *Raising the bar and closing the gap: Whatever it takes.* Bloomington, IN: Solution Tree Press.

Durlak, J. A., Weissberg, R. P., Dymnicki, A. B., Taylor, R. D., & Schellinger, K. B. (2011). The impact of enhancing students' social and emotional learning: A meta-analysis of school-based universal interventions. *Child Development, 82*(1), 405–432.

Education Commission of the States. (2013, June). *Better serving English language learners: A national imperative.* Presented at the National Forum on Education Policy, St. Louis, MO.

Elias, M. J., & Arnold, H. (Eds.). (2006). *The educator's guide to emotional intelligence and academic achievement: Social-emotional learning in the classroom.* Thousand Oaks, CA: Corwin Press.

Elias, M. J., Zins, J. E., Weissberg, R. P., Frey, K. S., Greenberg, M. T., Haynes, N. M., et al. (1997). *Promoting social and emotional learning: Guidelines for educators.* Alexandria, VA: Association for Supervision and Curriculum Development.

Fisher, D., Frey, N., & Lapp, D. (2008). Shared readings: Modeling comprehension, vocabulary, text structures, and text features for older readers. *The Reading Teacher, 61*(7), 548–557.

Flores, S. M., Batalova, J., & Fix, M. (2012). *The educational trajectories of English language learners in Texas.* Washington, DC: Migration Policy Institute. Accessed at www.migrationpolicy.org /research/educational-trajectories-english-language-learners-texason February 13, 2015.

Fountas, I. C., & Pinnell, G. S. (2001). *Guiding readers and writers, grades 3–6: Teaching comprehension, genre, and content literacy.* Portsmouth, NH: Heinemann.

Frederick County Public Schools. (n.d.). *Magnet summary directions (many variations!)*. Accessed at http://education.fcps.org/ths/sites/default/files/magnetsummarydirections1.pdf on February 17, 2015.

Gainesville City School System (n.d.). *Bloom's taxonomy process verbs, assessments, and questioning strategies* (Rev. ed.). Accessed at www.gcssk12.net/fullpanel/uploads/files/revised-blooms-chart.pdf on February 13, 2015.

Goleman, D. (1995). *Emotional intelligence*. New York: Bantam.

Graesser, A. C., Ozuru, Y., & Sullins, J. (2009). What is a good question? In M. G. McKeown & L. Kucan (Eds.), *Bringing reading research to life* (pp. 112–141). New York: Guilford.

Graham, S., & Perin, D. (2007). *Writing next: Effective strategies to improve writing of adolescents in middle and high schools*. Accessed at http://carnegie.org/fileadmin/Media/Publications/PDF/writingnext.pdf on May 22, 2015.

Graves, M., August, D., & Carlo, M. (2011). Teaching 50,000 words. *Better: Evidence-based Education, 3*(2), 6–7.

Grossman, A., Palmer, T., & Shoolroy, S. (2013). *Social emotional learning and the Common Core*. Accessed at http://coretaskproject.com/2013/01/22/social-emotional-learning-and-the-common-core on February 13, 2015.

Hargreaves, A., & Fullan, M. (Eds.). (2009). *Change wars*. Bloomington, IN: Solution Tree Press.

Hart, B., & Risley, T. R. (1995). *Meaningful differences in the everyday experience of young American children*. Baltimore: Brookes.

Haynes, M. (2012, October 31). *The role of language and literacy in college- and career-ready standards: Rethinking policy and practice in support of English language learners*. Washington, DC: Alliance for Excellent Education. Accessed at http://all4ed.org/reports-factsheets/the-role-of-language-and-literacy-in-college-and-career-ready-standards-rethinking-policy-and-practice-in-support-of-english-language-learners on February 13, 2015.

in2edu. (2003). *Bloom's taxonomy question generation charts: Task oriented question construction wheel and Bloom's taxonomy*. Austin, TX: Center for Teaching Excellence, Center for Teaching Excellence. Accessed at www.in2edu.com/resources/thinking_resources/blooms_taxonomy_chart.pdf on February 13, 2015.

Johnson, D. W., & Johnson, R. T. (1987). *Learning together and alone: Cooperative, competitive, and individualistic learning* (2nd ed.). Englewood Cliffs, NJ: Prentice-Hall.

Johnson, D. W., & Johnson R. T. (1991). *Learning together and alone: Cooperative, competitive, and individualistic learning* (3rd ed.). Englewood Cliffs, NJ: Prentice-Hall.

Joyce, B., & Calhoun, E. (2010). *Models of professional development: A celebration of educators*. Thousand Oaks, CA: Corwin Press.

Joyce, B., & Showers, B. (1983). *Power in staff development through research in training*. Alexandria, VA: Association for Supervision and Curriculum Development.

Joyce, B., & Showers, B. (2003). *Student achievement through staff development* (3rd ed.). Alexandria, VA: Association for Supervision and Curriculum Development.

Karchmer-Klein, R. (2015). *Lesson plan: Compare and contrast electronic text with traditionally printed text*. Accessed at www.readwritethink.org/classroom-resources/lesson-plans/compare-contrast -electronic-text-90.html on May 13, 2015.

Kifer, E. (1993). Opportunities, talents and participation. In L. Burstein (Ed.), *The IEA study of mathematics III: Student growth and classroom processes* (pp. 279–308). Oxford, England: Pergamon Press.

Kilpatrick, J., Swafford, J., & Findell, B. (Ed.). (2001). *Adding it up: Helping children learn mathematics—Report from the National Research Council*. Washington, DC: National Academies Press.

Kissner, E. (2011). *Text features* [Video file]. Accessed at www.slideshare.net/elkissn/text-features-6537031 on May 13, 2015.

Knight, J. (2011). *Unmistakable impact: A partnership approach for dramatically improving instruction*. Thousand Oaks, CA: Corwin Press.

Lee, O., Quinn, H., & Valdés, G. (2013). Science and language for English language learners in relation to Next Generation Science Standards and with implications for Common Core State Standards for English language arts and mathematics. *Educational Researcher, 42*(4), 223–233.

Linquanti, R. (2013, August 5). *Ensuring English learners' success with the Common Core and California's new ELD standards*. Paper presented at the California Teachers Association Summer Institute, Los Angeles, CA. Accessed at https://s3.amazonaws.com/pnmresources/pID-508 /topic-58305/462025889-Linquanti%20Session.pdf on February 13, 2015.

Luthar, S. S., & Becker, B. E. (2002). Privileged but pressured: A study of affluent youth. *Child Development, 73*(5), 1593–1610. Accessed at www.ncbi.nlm.nih.gov/pmc/articles /PMC3523355/ on July 28, 2015.

Marino, J. A. (n.d.). *Critical thinking: A lesson from the past on what matters*. Unpublished manuscript.

Marulis, L. M., & Neuman, S. B. (2010). The effects of vocabulary intervention on young children's world learning: A meta-analysis. *Review of Educational Research, 80*(3), 300–335.

Maryland Public Television. (2003). *Summarizing*. Accessed at www.thinkport.org/b52038ef-7cf2 –4c58–93a8-f531572739b7.asset on February 17, 2015.

Marzano, R. J. (2010). The art and science of teaching, summarizing to comprehend. *Reading to Learn, 67*(6), 83–84.

Marzano, R. J., & Pickering, D. J. (2010). *The highly engaged classroom*. Bloomington, IN: Marzano Research Laboratory.

Mathematical Sciences Education Board, the Board on Mathematical Sciences, & National Research Council. (Eds.). (1989). *Everybody counts: A report to the nation on the future of mathematics education*. Washington, DC: National Academies Press.

Mathews, G., Zeidner, M., & Roberts, R. D. (Eds.). (2007). *Emotional intelligence: Knowns and unknowns*. New York: Oxford University Press.

McCombs, B. L., & Whisler, J. S. (1997). *The learner-centered classroom and school: Strategies for increasing student motivation and achievement*. San Francisco: Jossey-Bass.

McTighe, J., & Wiggins, G. (2012). *From Common Core standards to curriculum: Five big ideas.* Accessed at http://grantwiggins.files.wordpress.com/2012/09/mctighe_wiggins_final_common _core_standards.pdf on February 13, 2015.

Meade PASS Training. (n.d.). *Summarizing strategies.* Accessed at www.meade.k12.sd.us/PASS /Pass%20Adobe%20Files/March%202007/SummarizingStrategies.pdf on February 17, 2015.

Milgrom-Elcott, T. (2013). Inspiring tomorrow's leaders. *Media Planet, 3*(2).

National Assessment of Educational Progress. (2013). The Nation's Report Card: National Student Groups-Science. Accessed at http://nationsreportcard.gov/science_2005/s0115.asp?tab _id=tab2&subtab_id=Tab_1&printver=#chart on July 20, 2015.

National Assessment of Educational Progress. (n.d.). *English language learners make gains at grades 4 and 8.* Accessed at http://nationsreportcard.gov/science_2005/s0115.asp?tab_id=tab2&subtab _id=Tab_1&printver=#chart on February 13, 2015.

National Center for Educational Statistics. (2009). *The nation's report card: Science 2009—National assessment of educational progress at grades 4, 8, and 12.* Accessed at www.nationsreportcard.gov /science_2009/science_2009_report on February 13, 2015.

National Center for Educational Statistics. (2012). *The nation's report card: Science 2011—National assessment of educational progress at grade 8.* Accessed at http://nces.ed.gov/nationsreportcard /pdf/main2011/2012465.pdf on February 13, 2015.

National Council of Teachers of Mathematics. (2012). *Principles and standards for school mathematics.* Accessed at www.nctm.org/uploadedFiles/Standards_and_Positions/CAEP _Standards/NCTM%20CAEP%20Standards%202012%20-%20Secondary.pdf on May 21, 2015.

National Governors Association Center for Best Practices & Council of Chief State School Officers. (2010a). *Common Core State Standards for English language arts and literacy in history/ social studies, science, and technical subjects.* Washington, DC: Authors. Accessed at www .corestandards.org/assets/CCSSI_ELA%20Standards.pdf on February 17, 2015.

National Governors Association Center for Best Practices & Council of Chief State School Officers. (2010b). *Common Core State Standards for English language arts & literacy in history / social studies, science, and technical subjects: Appendix A—Research supporting key elements of the standards.* Washington, DC: Author. Accessed at www.corestandards.org/assets/Appendix_A.pdf on February 17, 2015.

National Governors Association Center for Best Practices & Council of Chief State School Officers. (2010c). *Common Core State Standards for mathematics.* Washington, DC: Authors. Accessed at www.corestandards.org/assets/CCSSI_Math%20Standards.pdf on February 17, 2015.

National Governors Association Center for Best Practices & Council of Chief State School Officers. (2010d). *Reaching higher: The Common Core State Standards validation committee.* Accessed at www.corestandards.org/assets/CommonCoreReport_6.10.pdf on May 22, 2015.

National Governors Association Center for Best Practices & the Council of Chief State School Officers. (2010e). *Common Core State Standards initiative webinar.* Accessed at www.cesa9.k12 .wi.us/programs/ccss2.cfm.

National Reading Panel. (2000). *Teaching children to read: An evidence-based assessment of the scientific research literature on reading and its implications for reading instruction.* Washington, DC: National Institute of Child Health and Human Development.

National Research Council. (1989). *Everybody counts: A report to the nation on the future of mathematics education.* Washington, DC: National Academy Press.

Newkirk, T. (2010). The case for slow reading. *Educational Leadership, 67*(6), 6–11. Accessed at www.ascd.org/publications/educational-leadership/mar10/vol67/num06/The-Case-for-Slow -Reading.aspx on February 13, 2015.

NGSS Lead States. (2013). *Next Generation Science Standards: For states, by states.* Washington, DC: National Academies Press. Accessed at www.nextgenscience.org/next-generation-science -standards on July 20, 2015.

Orcutt, K. (n.d.). *Text structure frames.* Accessed at https://waecbrown.files.wordpress.com/2012/11 /textstructureframes-fullset.pdf on February 17, 2015.

Organisation for Economic Co-operation and Development. (2012). *Programme for International Student Assessment (PISA) results from PISA 2012: United States.* Accessed at www.oecd.org /unitedstates/PISA-2012-results-US.pdf on July 20, 2015.

Palincsar, A. S., & Brown, A. L. (1984). Reciprocal teaching of comprehension fostering and comprehension-monitoring activities. *Cognition and Instruction, 1*(2), 117–175.

Partnership for 21st Century Skills. (2014). *Framework for 21st century learning.* Washington, DC: Author. Accessed at www.p21.org/our-work/p21-framework on February 13, 2015.

Pew Research Center. (2007). *A portrait of "generation next": How young people view their lives, futures and politics—Summary of findings.* Washington, DC: Author. Accessed at www.people-press .org/2007/01/09/a-portrait-of-generation-next on February 13, 2015.

Peyton, J. K. (2013). *Human migration and global change: Why are people moving around? Does it matter?* Washington, DC: Calderón & Associates.

Pianta, R. (2007). *Teaching children well: New evidence-based approaches to teacher professional development and training.* Washington, DC: Center for American Progress.

Pink, D. (2005). *A whole new mind: Moving from the information age to the conceptual age.* New York: Riverhead Books.

Public Schools of North Carolina. (2010). *North Carolina Essential Standards: Social studies— American history course II.* Accessed at www.dpi.state.nc.us/docs/acre/standards/new-standards /social-studies/american-history-2.pdf on May 12, 2015.

Riley, R. W. (1997). *Mathematics equals opportunity.* Washington, DC: U.S. Department of Education.

Rotherham, A. J., & Willingham, D. (2009). 21st century skills: The challenges ahead. *Educational Leadership, 67*(1), 16–21.

Sanders, B. (2012). *Highlighting strategies for student success.* Sacramento: California Office to Reform Education.

Sanchez, N. (2013). *Common Core State Standards.* Accessed at http://ctaipd.ning.com/page /common-core-state-standards on February 13, 2015.

Schaps, E., Battistich, V., & Solomon, D. (2004). Community in school as key to student growth: Findings from the child development project. In J. E. Zins, R. P. Weissberg, M. C. Wang, & H. J. Walberg (Eds.), *Building academic success on social and emotional learning: What does the research say?* (pp. 189–205). New York: Teachers College Press.

Shanahan, T. (2012, July 12). *Planning for close reading.* Accessed at www.shanahanonliteracy.com/2012/07/planning-for-close-reading.html on February 13, 2015.

Shanahan, T. (2013, Fall). Letting the text take center stage: How the Common Core State Standards will transform English language arts instruction. *American Educator.* Accessed at www.aft.org/pdfs/americaneducator/fall2013/Shanahan.pdf on February 13, 2015.

Sheehy, K. (2012). High school students not prepared for college, career. *U.S. News and World Report Education.* Accessed at www.usnews.com/education/blogs/high-school-notes/2012/08/22/high-school-students-not-prepared-for-college-career on February 13, 2015.

Shorser, L. (2013). *Bloom's taxonomy interpreted for mathematics.* Accessed at www.math.toronto.edu/writing/BloomsTaxonomy.pdf on February 13, 2015.

Short, D. J., & Fitzsimmons, S. (2007). *Double the work: Challenges and solutions to acquiring language and academic literacy for adolescent English language learners.* Washington, DC: Alliance for Excellent Education.

Simon, S. (2006). *Volcanoes.* New York: HarperCollins.

Slavin, R. E., & Madden, N. A. (2001). *One million children: Success for all.* Thousand Oaks, CA: Corwin Press.

Slavin, R. E., Madden, N. A., Calderón, M. E., Chamberlain, A., & Hennessy, M. (2011). Reading and language outcomes of a five-year randomized evaluation of transitional bilingual education. *Educational Evaluation and Policy Analysis, 33*(1), 47–58.

Snow, C., & Biancarosa, G. (2003). *Adolescent literacy and the achievement gap: What do we know and where do we go from here?* (Carnegie Corporation of New York Adolescent Literacy Funders Meeting Report). Accessed at http://olms1.cte.jhu.edu/olms/data/resource/2029/class9_snow_biancarosa.pdf on February 13, 2015.

STEM Education Coalition. (2012). *Statement of core policy principles.* Accessed at www.stemedcoalition.org/wp-content/uploads/2012/04/Note-STEM-Education-Coalition-Core-Principles-2012.pdf on June 24, 2015.

Teaching Effectiveness Program. (n.d.). *Bloom's taxonomy of cognitive levels.* Accessed at http://tep.uoregon.edu/resources/assessment/multiplechoicequestions/blooms.html on February 13, 2015.

Thomas, W. P., & Collier, V. P. (2002). *A national study of school effectiveness for language minority students' long-term academic achievement.* Washington, DC: National Clearinghouse for English Language Acquisition Resource Collection Series.

U.S. Department of Education. (2013a). *President's FY2014 budget request for the U.S. Department of Education.* Accessed at www2.ed.gov/about/overview/budget/budget14/index.html on February 13, 2015.

U.S. Department of Education. (2013b). *Total number of English learners: 2010–2011.* Accessed at http://eddataexpress.ed.gov/data-elements.cfm on February 13, 2015.

Van Lier, L., & Walqui, A. (2013). *Language and the Common Core State Standards: Understanding language series.* Stanford, CA: Stanford University.

World-Class Instructional Design and Assessment Consortium. (2012). *2012 amplification of the English language development standards, kindergarten–grade 12.* Accessed at www.wida.us/get .aspx?id=540 on February 13, 2015.

Wormeli, R. (2005). *Summarization in any subject: 50 techniques to improve student learning.* Alexandria, VA: Association for Supervision and Curriculum Development. Accessed at http://books.google.com/books?id=ZTL1LP6SitAC&printsec=frontcover&source=gbs_ge _summary_r&cad=0#v=onepage&q&f=false on February 13, 2015.

Yaron, L. (2011). *Empowering youth, meeting the challenge* [Web log post]. Accessed at www.ed.gov /blog/2011/02/educator-toolkit-for-2011-national-financial-capability-challenge/on February 13, 2015.

Zins, J., Payton, J. W., Weissberg R. P., & O'Brien, M. U. (2007). Social and emotional learning and successful school performance. In G. Matthews, M. Zeidner, & R. D. Roberts (Eds.), *Emotional intelligence: Knowns and unknowns* (pp. 376–395). New York: Oxford University Press.

Zins, J. E., Weissberg, R. P., Wang, M. C., & Walberg, H. J. (Eds.). (2004). *Building academic success on social and emotional learning: What does the research say?* New York: Teachers College Press.

INDEX

Breaking Through
Edited by Margarita Espino Calderón
Utilizing new research and field studies, this book provides a whole-school approach to helping English learners achieve academically while they learn English. Discover why ELs learn better when language, literacy, and subject matter are integrated, and learn how to prepare all teachers in a school to meet the needs of this growing student population.
BKF552

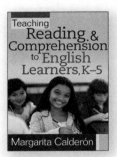

Teaching Reading & Comprehension to English Learners, K–5
Margarita Espino Calderón
As more English learners enroll in school each year, teachers and administrators are concerned with the large gap in reading and academic standing between ELs and students performing at grade level. This book addresses the language, literacy, and content instructional needs of ELs and frames quality instruction within effective schooling structures and the implementation of RTI.
BKF402

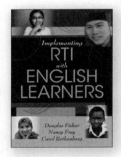

Implementing RTI With English Learners
Douglas Fisher, Nancy Frey, and Carol Rothenberg
Learn why RTI is the ideal framework for supporting English learners. Follow the application and effectiveness of RTI through classroom examples and the stories of four representative students of varying ages, nationalities, and language proficiency levels.
BKF397

Teaching Reading & Comprehension to English Learners, K–5: Online Course
Margarita Espino Calderón
Calderón outlines techniques for elementary teachers seeking to improve the reading and comprehension skills of ELs in their classrooms. You will be led through the steps needed to select vocabulary for reading, preteach this vocabulary, and model comprehension strategies like think-alouds and partner reading.
KDS020

Solution Tree | Press

a division of

Solution Tree

Visit solution-tree.com or call 800.733.6786 to order.

Wait! Your professional development journey doesn't have to end with the last pages of this book.

We realize improving student learning doesn't happen overnight. And your school or district shouldn't be left to puzzle out all the details of this process alone.

No matter where you are on the journey, we're committed to helping you get to the next stage.

Take advantage of everything from **custom workshops** to **keynote presentations** and **interactive web and video conferencing**. We can even help you develop an action plan tailored to fit your specific needs.

Let's get the conversation started.

Call 888.763.9045 today.

solution-tree.com